F. W. E

M000206018

Life
Verses

The Bible's Impact on Famous Lives

• Volume Three •

kregel
PUBLICATIONS

Grand Rapids, MI 49501

Life Verses: The Bible's Impact on Famous Lives, Vol. Three by F.W. Boreham.

Published in 1994 by Kregel Publications, a division of Kregel, Inc., P.O. Box 2607, Grand Rapids, MI 49501. Kregel Publications provides trusted, biblical publications for Christian growth and service. Your comments and suggestions are valued.

Cover Design & Artwork: © Tammy Johnson,
Flat River Graphics

Library of Congress Cataloging-in-Publication Data
[A casket of cameos]
Boreham, Frank W. (Frank William), 1871-1959.
   Life verses: The Bible's impact on famous lives, vol. three / Frank William Boreham.
       p.   cm. (Great text series)
   Originally published: A casket of cameos. London: Epworth Press, 1924.
   1. Christian biography. 2. Bible—Influence. I. Title. II. Series: Boreham, F.W. (Frank William), 1871-1959. Great text series.
BR1702.B615   1994   270'.092—dc20   93-37490
                           [B]   CIP
ISBN 0-8254-2168-3 (paperback)

       1 2 3 4 5 Printing / Year 98 97 96 95 94

Printed in the United States of America

CONTENTS

FOREWORD

When Frank Boreham was four months old, he was on an outing with his nurse when a Gypsy caravan passed by, and an old Gypsy woman, noticing the child, came over to them. She looked at the little boy's hand and said to the nurse, "Tell his mother to put a pen in his hand, and he'll never want for a living." The prophecy proved true. Boreham became one of the world's most prolific religious writers with more than fifty books to his credit, not to speak of hundreds of newspaper and magazine articles and essays.

As the boy grew up, he was introduced to both the things of the Spirit and the things of the mind. Faithful Christian parents saw to it that he was trained in the Word of God and also that he learned to appreciate good reading. Frank's father, noticing that Frank was reading some shallow novels, introduced him to the vast treasures of biography, and the boy was "hooked for life."

In 1891 he united with the Kenyon Baptist Church in Brixton, of which the pastor, James Douglas, was a good friend of C. H. Spurgeon. When the pastor discovered that Boreham was considering the ministry, he naturally urged him to apply to Spurgeon's Pastor's College. Boreham did, and he was the last student that Spurgeon personally selected before his lamented death.

In 1894 Thomas Spurgeon returned to London after ministering in New Zealand, and he brought with him a request for a pastor from a new church at Mosgiel.

The college staff decided that Boreham was their man. He served in Mosgiel, New Zealand; Hobart, Tasmania; and Armadale, Australia; and then he traveled to many lands and preached to vast congregations. Where he was unable to travel personally, his books carried his messages.

The story behind this unique, five-volume series is this: Boreham was about to begin a Sunday evening series when it dawned upon him that a series on alternate Sunday evenings would encourage the congregation to return week after week. As if by inspiration, it came to him to preach on "Texts That Made History." He announced that the next Sunday evening he would preach on "Martin Luther's Text." Little did he realize that these sermons would continue for 125 Sunday evenings and attract more interest and win more people to Christ than any other series he ever preached.

If at first Boreham does not excite you, give him time. He grows on you. He has a way of touching the nerve centers of life and getting to that level of reality that too often we miss. There is something for everybody in a Boreham book because his writing touches on the unchanging essentials of life, not the passing accidentals; we need this emphasis today.

WARREN W. WIERSBE

Adapted from *Walking with the Giants*, by Warren W. Wiersbe. Copyright 1976, Baker Book House Company. Used by permission.

INTRODUCTION

THE stately lives of noble men, are they not the glory of the whole earth?

They are the streams that, transforming every dusty desert into a fruitful field or a garden of roses, fill the world with life and loveliness.

In this book—and its predecessors of the same series—I have simply traced these sparkling waters to their secret source and fountain-head far up among the everlasting hills.

FRANK W. BOREHAM

Armadale, Victoria, Australia

1

GEORGE MOORE'S TEXT
1806–1876
English merchant and philanthropist.

John 5:24

I

SHALL I ever forget the night on which I looked for
the first time on the *Life of George Moore, Merchant
and Philanthropist,* by Samuel Smiles? I was only
a small boy at the time, yet the memory of it rushes
back so vividly upon me that it seems impossible
that, since then, so many years have flown. I had,
a few months earlier, made a most sensational discovery—the discovery of the possibilities of a circu-
lating library. My schoolfellow, Gilbert Finch, a boy
of about my own age, had introduced me to a dingy
little schoolroom, not far from my home, where, in
return for the modest outlay of a penny a month, I
could borrow as many tales of adventure as I could
manage to devour. When I reflect on the hordes of
cannibals, Red Indians, brigands, pirates and smugglers that I obtained in exchange for that first penny,
I catch myself wondering whether, in the entire history of finance, one solitary copper coin was ever
made to go so far. In every spare minute, from daylight to dark, I curled myself up in my father's capacious armchair and lost myself among the grizzly

bears of the Rocky Mountains, the boa-constrictors of the Amazon, the wolves of Siberia, the whales of the Indian Ocean, the elephants of Africa and the tigers of Bengal. I romped through Ballantyne and Marryat, Mayne Reid and Fenimore Cooper in no time. I wondered how I had contrived to fill in the dreary days of human existence before the little library was revealed to me. And then, just as my fevered brain was becoming one confused jumble of Indian wigwams, Arab tents, Zulu kraals, Arctic snow-huts and smugglers' caves, my father suddenly took it into his head that such an unmixed diet of wild excitement was not conducive to the best intellectual development. He urged me to try a change; and, from some more sedate library that he himself patronized, he brought me the *Life of George Moore*. I glanced through it, but could see no sign of a shipwreck or a slave-raid or a scalp-hunt anywhere. Still, I felt that, since my father provided me with the pennies that brought me such torrents of enjoyment from my own library, it was due to him that I should make an honest attempt to sample his. I read the ponderous volume from cover to cover, and, to my astonishment, it filled me with a delight of which, in anticipation, I had never dreamed. After an interval of forty years, I have read the book again, and every incident seems wonderfully familiar. I owe to that childish experience a penchant for biography that has deepened, rather than evaporated, with the years.

II

This brawling little burn, that winds its way in and out among the alders and the willows of this green, green valley, is the Dowbeck. It is hurrying excitedly down the glen that it may throw itself with a laugh into the waters of the River Ellen. That glorious old mansion on the hillside—with masses of cream-colored roses clustering luxuriantly over its walls, and thousands of lilies flecking, like snow-flakes, the yew hedge that divides the garden from the bowling-green—is 'Whitehall,' the home of George Moore. The house is surrounded by un-dulating lawns, winding walks, well-kept flower-beds, and graceful shrubberies. In the old days of Border warfare it played a great part in the history of the countryside; it even figures prominently in one of Sir Walter Scott's romances. Not far away, over the hill yonder, is the tiny village of Mealsgate, where George Moore was born. How little he dreamed in the old days when, as a poor boy, he fished in the Ellen and ransacked the wide chimney of 'Whitehall,' in search of jackdaws' eggs, that, one day, this magnificent estate would be his very own!

And here is the man himself, enjoying, in com-pany with his big bulldog 'Jack,' one of those rambles of which he is so fond! He is a striking figure, sturdy and massive. In his youth he was one of the best wrestlers in the country. His whole aspect impresses you as that of a man of blunt frankness, robust character and indomitable energy. His alert brown eyes, eager and penetrating, have an emphatically dauntless look. His mouth, too, is firm and powerful. His fine head, with its abundance of curly hair, is set squarely upon his shoulders. You feel that you are in the presence of a strong man and a good one.

III

In his younger days George Moore was a commercial traveller; and he revelled in the society of commercial travellers to the end of his life. In the interests of his firm he visited every town of importance in Great Britain and America. But the most remarkable of his travels was undertaken in his forty-fifth year, for in that year he made the greatest journey that any man can make. He *passed from death unto life!* The extraordinary thing about George Moore is that he did not begin his spiritual pilgrimage until he was at the zenith of his powers and at the climax of his illustrious career. Before his need of a Saviour pressed itself at all urgently upon him, he had been ten years married, had become a partner in his firm, and established his position in life, had been invited by the Lord Mayor of London to become Sheriff of the city, had been offered an important seat in Parliament, and had earned a great reputation for philanthropy.

The story of his spiritual experience, carefully

recorded, was found among his papers after his death. In the first part of his life, he says, he had *no time to think*. 'At night I tumbled into bed without asking God's blessing, and I was generally so tired that I fell asleep in a few minutes.' *'No time to think!'* This, doubtless, was his general condition; but to that general rule there were notable exceptions, *three* particularly.

There was *one* never-to-be-forgotten occasion on which he spent the whole night thinking. It was the night after his mother's funeral. He was only six at the time. As soon as they told him that his mother was dead, he was filled with curiosity and dread. *What had happened to her?* He timidly crept to her bedside; uncovered the cold, white face; touched it; spoke to her; and was puzzled by her icy indifference. On the night after the funeral he slept with his father in the bed from which his mother's body had just been taken. He was frightened, startled, horror-stricken. *Where was she?* He never once closed his eyes; and, to the last day of his life, that terrifying experience haunted his memory. That night was certainly an exception. That night he thought. He thought of life; he thought of death; he thought, in his childish way, of immortality.

There was *another* occasion on which he thought. It was during his apprenticeship at Wigton. He became enslaved by the gambling habit and often sat at the card-table till the grey and ghostly dawn came stealing through the windows. One early morning—it was the morning of Christmas Day— he returned to his room to find that he had been locked out. By dint of climbing over roofs and chimneys—an art which he had acquired when searching for jackdaws' eggs—he managed to gain entrance to his room through the window. He slipped into bed; but not to sleep. For very soon the waits came round, singing the Christmas carols. 'The sweet music awoke me to a sense of my wrong-doing. I felt overwhelmed with penitence and remorse. I thought of my dear father and feared that I might break his heart and bring down his grey hairs in sorrow to the grave.' He remained in bed all day—*thinking!* 'I resolved,' he says, 'to give up card-playing and gambling,' and, true to his pledge, he never again touched a card or hazarded a coin.

The *third* occasion on which he thought was in his forty-fifth year. It suddenly occurred to him that neither his great success, nor his immense popularity, nor his princely benefactions could atone for his sins or blot out a certain inner defilement of which he was becoming increasingly conscious. 'I am pain-fully aware,' he says, 'of the depravity of my own heart.' It worried him; the anxiety of it kept him awake at night; he would rise in the darkness, kneel in anguish by his bedside, and pray for deliverance. 'For the last two years,' he says, 'I have been earnestly asking God to give me some sudden change of heart; but no sudden change comes.' With bitter tears he sought the way of repentance, but, like Esau, could not find it. 'It seems,' he moaned, 'as if God has hidden His face from me.' And then, like a flash, the light broke upon him, and all his wretchedness was gone.

IV

It was *a text* that did it. It suddenly occurred to him that he had been confusing the salvation of his soul with the arrival of certain moods, feelings and sensations. Because no rush of ecstasy had swept into his heart, he had taken it for granted that God had turned a deaf ear to his piteous cries and passionate entreaties. He saw his mistake.

'I am determined for the future,' he says, 'not to perplex my mind with seeking for some extraordinary impressions, signs, or tokens of the new birth. I believe the gospel. I love the Lord Jesus Christ. I receive with confidence the promise that *He that heareth My word, and believeth on Him that sent Me, hath everlasting life, and shall not come into condemnation, but is passed from death unto life.*' He rested implicitly on that promise and entered into peace.

George Moore's testimony reminds me of Frank Bullen's experience with the same text. It was in the old sail-loft at Port Chalmers, in New Zealand. Little Mr. Falconer, the sailors' missionary, had conducted an evangelistic service. Frank Bullen, then a sailor-lad, was impressed, and remained behind for further conversation. Mr. Falconer quoted to him the promise on which George Moore had rested with such confidence.

'Verily, verily, I say unto you, He that heareth My word, and believeth on Him that sent Me, hath everlasting life, and shall not come into condemnation, but is passed from death unto life.'

Frank Bullen said that he believed; yet his belief brought him no assurance of deliverance.

'Ah, I see how it is,' exclaimed Mr. Falconer, 'you are waiting for the witness of *your feelings* to the truth of Him who is Himself the Truth. You dare not take Him at His word unless your feelings, which are subject to a thousand changes a day, corroborate it. You must *believe Him* in spite of your feelings and act accordingly.'

'In a moment,' says Frank Bullen, in telling the story years afterwards, 'in a moment the hidden mystery was made clear to me, and I said quietly, "I see, sir; it is the credibility of God against the witness of my feelings. Then *I believe God!*" "Let us thank God," answered the little man; and together we knelt down by the bench. Little more was said. There was no extravagant joy, no glorious bursting into light and liberty such as I have read about as happening on these occasions; it was just the satisfaction of having found one's way after long groping in darkness and misery.'

That was George Moore's experience exactly.

And, when I see this stately *'Verily, Verily'* opening the door of deliverance to this simple sailor-lad on one side of the world, and to this great merchant and philanthropist on the other, I feel that there are none among the sons of men to whom it will deny its emancipating ministry.

'He that believeth,' says the text. George Moore believed and he kept on believing. 'The foremost feature in his character,' the biography tells us, 'was the admirable simplicity of his faith.' And, in his own diary, I come upon entries such as these:

'Every day I feel more and more my own unworthiness. I have nothing to rest upon but Christ; yet surely that is enough for me!'

'Just as I am, without one plea—a poor, unworthy sinner. Christ takes me as I am, without money or price or works. My works are nothing.'

Such a change had the text wrought! He made Mrs. Moore promise—and he often reminded her of her pledge—that, if she was with him when he was dying, she would repeat the words to him:

'Verily, verily, I say unto you, He that heareth My word, and believeth on Him that sent Me, hath everlasting life, and shall not come into condemnation, but is passed from death unto life.'

V

The text transfigured everything. It even transfigured his philanthropy. He always revelled in giving away his money. Every New Year's Day,

as he started a new pocket book, he inscribed upon
the flyleaf the lines:

> What I spent, I had:
> What I saved, I lost:
> What I gave, I have.

He began each year by sending large cheques to
the charities and organizations in which he was
interested, many of which he had himself inaugurated. He enjoyed giving. 'If the world only knew
half the happiness that a man has in doing good,' he
used to say, 'it would do a great deal more.' And,
when he first began to feel his need of a Saviour, he
would add: "I wish that my *faith* were as strong
as my *works!*'

And, when *faith* came, his *works* were glorified by
its coming. It gave to all his activities a new and
higher motive. He hung in his smokeroom an illu-
minated tablet on which was inscribed the thirteenth
chapter of Paul's First Epistle to the Corinthians—
the chapter that magnifies the glory of love. In large
bright letters at the head of the tablet were the
words:

CHARITY NEVER FAILETH,

and, at the foot:

NOW ABIDETH FAITH.

Those two inscriptions are very significant. George
Moore's later life represents the wedding of Faith
to Charity. He felt that it was not enough to give
money and to give it lavishly. 'I believe,' he said, in

addressing a great public meeting at Aldersgate Street, 'I believe that mere money, unless it be given for the love of Jesus, is as filthy rags in the sight of God.' He therefore felt it his duty to give it in such a way that those for whose benefit it was designed were made aware of the love that prompted it. He was not content to post cheques to treasurers. In spite of the protests of his friends, who thought it undignified for a rich city merchant to mingle with the raggedness and filth of the slums, he went fearlessly and familiarly among the thieves, tramps and vagrants who herded in London's squalor. 'I feel,' he explained, 'that nothing can reach to the depth of human misery, or heal such sorrow, but the love of Jesus, the Good Shepherd who yearned over such people with infinite pity and gave His life for His lost sheep.'

VI

The carriage is at the door. George Moore, now a man of seventy, is driving off to preside at a meeting of the Nurses' Institution. 'What,' he asked his wife, as he bade her good-bye, 'what is that passage that I want to quote? Oh, I remember—*"Well done, good and faithful servant, enter thou into the joy of thy Lord."* ' But that speech was never to be delivered. He was knocked down by a pair of runaway horses. Mrs. Moore hurried to the inn in which he was dying, and, bending over him, quoted the text in accordance with her promise.

'Verily, verily, I say unto you, He that heareth My word, and believeth on Him that sent Me, hath everlasting life, and shall not come into condemnation, but is passed from death unto life.'

'He looked wistfully into my face,' says Mrs. Moore, 'and he told me that he was not afraid; his Saviour would never leave him nor forsake him. Several times afterwards he spoke to me, expressing the same trust. He knew perfectly well that he was dying; but his faith failed not.'

'From death unto life!'

'Well done, good and faithful servant, enter thou into the joy of thy Lord!'

He intended to have quoted the words to others; the programme was altered; and he went to hear them addressed to himself!

2

DAVID BRAINERDS'S TEXT
1718–1747
Pioneer missionary to the American Indians.

John 7:37

I

IT is a thickly-wooded solitude beside a graceful inlet of the Susquehanna. The dense and matted vegetation stands as it has stood from the foundation of the world. The silence of the wilderness is broken only by the lapping of the mimic wavelets and the flapping of the wings of the waterfowl. On the mossy bank near the water's edge sits a white man, a mere youth—the palest of palefaces—with his Bible on his knee. Have a good look at him; he is a man in a million; he did more than any other to usher in the world's new day. He is the morning star of the missionary movement. He is a tall spare youth, of almost feminine face, and large, sad, lustrous eyes. It is a lovely evening in the early summer of 1744; and, only a few yards from him, a colony of beavers is building a dam across the stream. Looking up from the open page before him, he watches the clever little creatures at their task. They have no more idea that they are observed than he knows that he is being watched by wolfish eyes concealed within the impenetrable foliage. The red men, as silent and as sinewy as serpents, follow him everywhere and mark his every step. It is well for him that they do.

For, on his very first journey to the Forks of the Delaware, the insatiable curiosity of the Indians saved his life. He had been told of a particularly ferocious tribe, living far back in the forests of New Jersey, and he determined to take the gospel to them. When, towards evening, he saw the smoke of their camp fires, he pitched his tent and resolved to enter the settlement in the morning. He had been led to expect a hostile reception, but, to his indescribable astonishment, the whole tribe came out to meet him as, soon after sunrise, he approached the wigwams. The reverence that they exhibited almost took his breath away. He only learned later that, during the night that he had spent on the outskirts of the village, their sharp eyes had been constantly upon him. As soon as it was whispered that a white man was coming through the woods, a party of warriors had gone forth to kill him. But, when they drew near to his tent, they saw the paleface on his knees. And, even whilst he prayed, a rattlesnake crept to his side, lifted its ugly head as if to strike, flicked its forked tongue almost in his face, and then, without any apparent reason, glided swiftly away into the brushwood. 'The Great Spirit is with the paleface!' the Indians said; and they accorded him a prophet's welcome.

But we have digressed. We left David Brainerd sitting under a broad-leafed basswood tree, watching the beavers in the river below.   Something has frightened the beavers now, and they have vanished; perhaps they caught a glimpse of the white man or of the Indians among the trees. At any rate, they have gone; and, now that he has nothing to distract him, his eyes are fastened once more upon the Bible on his knee. It lies open at the page that is more thumbed than any other. To it he always turns in moments of great loneliness or great anxiety or great depression. He is reading from the seventh of John. *In the last day, that great day of the feast, Jesus stood and cried, saying, If any man thirst, let him come unto Me and drink.* Whilst David Brainerd, a youth of twenty-six, sat beside that lonely western stream, John Wesley, in the prime of life, was stirring England as England had never been stirred before. In some respects they were twin souls, although the one died at twenty-nine, whilst the other lived to be nearly ninety. One of Brainerd's biographers has said of him that 'he belonged to a class of men who seem to be chosen of heaven to illustrate the sublime possibilities of Christian attainment; men of seraphic fervor of devotion; men whose one overmastering passion is to win souls for Christ and to become wholly like Him themselves.' To this heroic class John Wesley also belonged. He recognized his spiritual kinship. 'What can be done,' he asked his English Conference, 'what can be done to revive the work of God where it has decayed?' And he answered his own question by replying: 'Let every preacher read carefully the *Life of David Brainerd!*' To-day, *Wesley's Journal* and *Brainerd's Journal* stand side by side among our choicest classics of devotion. In his early days John Wesley devoted himself to the evangelization of the Red Indians: David Brainerd spent all his ministerial days among them. Mr. Wesley used to say that, whenever the cravings of his soul became so intense that no satisfaction could be found, even at earth's purest fountains, he invariably found comfort in that sublime proclamation: *If any man thirst, let him come unto Me and drink!*

'*Come!*' cried the Saviour in the temple courts. '*Come unto Me!*'

'*If any man thirst, let him come unto Me and drink!*'

John Wesley and David Brainerd never saw each other's faces; it may be that, until after Brainerd's death, Mr. Wesley never so much as heard his young contemporary's name; the Atlantic rolled between them, and their fields lay far apart; but, in their affection for the Saviour's stupendous proclamation at the Feast of Tabernacles, their twin hearts beat as one.

II

David Brainerd only lived to be twenty-nine; yet, during that brief career of his, he assumed three separate and distinct relationships towards the text.

There was a time when the text *irritated* him. It

is his own word. He was reared in a Puritan home in Connecticut, and was left an orphan at fourteen. As a little boy he was extraordinarily serious, and startled his elders by asking the most grave and searching questions. 'I was from my youth somewhat sober and inclined to melancholy,' his *Journal* tells us, 'but do not remember anything of conviction of sin, worthy of remark, till I was seven or eight years of age.' Then began a period of darkness and distress which, though varying in intensity, lasted until he was a youth of twenty-one. At about that age he was walking one morning in a solitary place when, as he says, he was brought to a sudden stand. He felt like a man reeling on the edge of a precipice. 'It seemed to me,' he says, 'that I was totally lost.' Mr. Stoddart's *Guide to Christ* fell into his hands; but, as he says, it only *irritated* him. He felt angry with the author. For, although the book described with scientific accuracy the terrible distress which he was himself experiencing, it did not satisfactorily explain to him the way of deliverance. It told him to come to Christ. *'If any man thirst, let him come unto Me and drink!'* But what, precisely, did Mr. Stoddart mean? What, precisely, did the Saviour mean? 'Whilst I was in this distressed, bewildered and tumultuous state of mind, I was *irritated*,' he writes, 'through not being able to find out what faith was. What was it to believe? What was it to come to Christ? I read the calls of Christ to the weary and the heavy-laden, but

could find *no way* that He directed me to come in.
I thought that I would gladly come, if I only knew
how.   Mr. Stoddart's book told me to come to
Christ, but did not tell me anything that I could *do*
that would bring me to Him.   For,' he significantly
adds, 'I was not yet effectually and experimentally
taught that there could be no way prescribed, whereby a *natural* man could, of his own strength, obtain
that which is *supernatural,* and which the highest
angel cannot give.'

And so the text, coming to him the first time,
brought no comfort.   It only awoke 'a great inward
opposition.'   It *irritated* him.

III

Happily, the text repeated its visit.   God gives
second knocks.   Again the Saviour stood and cried,
as He cried on the great day of the feast, *If any man
thirst, let him come unto Me and drink.*   And this
time the text *captivated* him.   Again, it is his own
word.   It was a Sunday evening—the evening of
July 12, 1739.   He was walking in the same solitary
place.   'At this time,' he says, 'the way of salvation
opened to me with such infinite wisdom, suitableness
and excellency that I wondered that I should ever
have desired any other way of salvation.   I was
amazed that I had not dropped my own contrivances
and complied with this lovely, blessed and excellent
way before.   If I could have been saved by my
own duties, or any other way that I had formerly

conceived, my whole soul would now have refused it. I wondered that all the world did not see and comply with this way of salvation.'

'*If any man thirst*'—it is the only condition.

'*Let him come unto Me*'—it is the only command.

'*Let him come unto Me and drink!*'—it is the only satisfaction that a thirsty man desires.

And David Brainerd was a thirsty man. You can scarcely find a paragraph in his *Journal* in which the symbolism of the parched tongue does not occur. 'I felt my soul hungering and thirsting.' 'I hungered and thirsted, but was not refreshed and satisfied.' 'My soul longed for God, the living God.' 'I thirsted night and day for a closer acquaintance with Him.' Such phrases punctuate every page.

'*I longed!*' '*I longed!*' '*I longed!*'

'*I thirsted!*' '*I thirsted!*' '*I thirsted!*'

'*If any man thirst, let him come unto Me and drink!*'

Brainerd thirsted: Brainerd came; Brainerd drank! He left that solitary retreat of his that day singing in his soul the song that, a century later, Horatius Bonar reduced to language:

> I heard the voice of Jesus say,
>   'Behold, I freely give
> The living water; thirsty one,
>   Stoop down, and drink and live.'
> I came to Jesus, and I drank
>   Of that life-giving stream;
> My thirst was quenched, my soul revived,
>   And now I live in Him.

'Unspeakable glory seemed,' he says, 'to open to the view and apprehension of my soul. I do not mean any external brightness, for I saw no such thing. It was a new view of God such as I had never had before. I stood still, wondered and admired. I had never before seen anything comparable to it for excellency and beauty; it was widely different from all the conceptions that ever I had had of God or things divine. I felt myself in a new world, and everything about me appeared with a different aspect from what it was wont to do. My soul was *captivated* and delighted. I rejoiced with joy unspeakable.'

'That,' says President Jonathan Edwards, in pointing to this entry in the *Journal*, 'that is the story of Brainerd's conversion. It was not a mere confirmation of certain moral principles: it was entirely a supernatural work, turning him at once from darkness to marvellous light, and from the power of sin to the dominion of holiness.' 'The change he then experienced was,' the President says again, 'the greatest change that ever he knew.' It transfigured his whole life.

And so the text that, on its first appearance, *irritated* him, came again, and, at its second coming, *captivated* him. 'I was completely *captivated!*' he joyously exclaims.

IV

But there was a *third* phase. The words that first

irritated and then *captivated* him, at length *animated* his whole being.

As soon as the burning thirst of his own soul had been divinely slaked, it occurred to him that such thirst was no monopoly of his. The text as good as said so.

'*If any man thirst!*'

'*Any man!*' '*Any man!*' '*Any man!*'

'*If any man thirst, let him come unto Me and drink!*'

Brainerd seemed to be looking out upon a thirsty world. His lot was cast in an age that knew nothing of missionary enterprise. Our great societies were yet unborn. For the evangelization of the world no prayers were offered and no money given. It was through reading Brainerd's *Life,* in accordance with Mr. Wesley's counsel, that William Carey caught his vision and threw open the doors of a new day. It was Brainerd's biography that made Henry Martyn a missionary. Brainerd was a leader, a pathfinder, a pioneer; he blazed the trail. 'His story,' as Mr. J. M. Sherwood says, 'proves him to be one of the most illustrious characters of modern times; it has done more to develop and mould the spirit of modern missions, and to fire the heart of the Christian church, than that of any other man since the apostolic age. One such personage, one such character, is a greater power in human history than a finite mind can calculate.'

He longed to tell the whole wide world of the

Saviour's cry: *'If any man thirst, let him come unto Me and drink!'* But how could he? China, India, Africa—all these were out of the question. He thought of the heathen that haunted the prairies and forests of his own land. He was scarcely more than a boy, and he felt the fascination that youth has always felt for the distinctive and picturesque features of Indian life. He thought of the canoes and the wigwams; the mats and the moccasins, the frayed leggings and the feathered head-gear, the bows and the quivers, the scalping-knives and the tomahawks, the pow-wows and the peace-pipes; he thought of these, and he thought, above all, of the man himself. He thought of the Indian's haughty and taciturn demeanor, of his lithe and agile movement, of his simple but dignified eloquence, of his courage and resourcefulness of the warpath, and of his poetic and imaginative accomplishments in time of peace. David Brainerd made up his mind that the Indian was well worth winning, and he devoted his young life to the conquest.

He was not mistaken in supposing that others were thirsty as well as he. Again and again in his *Journal* he speaks of the hunger of the tribes for the message that he took them. He tells how an Iroquois woman confessed that, from the moment at which she first heard him, her whole heart had cried out for the gospel. To a great assembly of tattooed warriors he preaches on *'Herein is love, not that we loved God, but that He loved us and sent*

His Son to be the propitiation for our sins.' 'There were scarce three in forty,' he says, 'that could refrain from tears, and the more I discoursed of the love and compassion of God in sending His Son to suffer for the sins of men, the more they wept.' And he tells of another occasion on which, when he uncovered the communion-table and explained the significance of the sacred mysteries, the whole company was dissolved in tears.

And so this frail young consumptive, racked with his cough and never free from pain, passed from tribe to tribe, telling everywhere the story of the Cross. Groping his way through dense and trackless forests, he spent most of his days in the saddle, startling the creatures of the wild as he broke upon their age-long solitudes. Most of his nights he spent beneath the open sky. Frail as was his frame, he exposed himself to perils and privations of every kind. Yet, as Mr. Sherwood says, he never wavered in his purpose, never regretted his choice, and never paused in his task until, after five brief but strenuous years, he rode back to New England to die.

And the text, still holding its old place in his heart, was ever on his tongue. It ever impelled him to fresh conquests. Here are a few extracts from the *Journal:*

Feb. 15, 1745. This evening I was much assisted in meditating on that precious text: *Jesus stood and cried, If any man thirst, let him come unto Me and drink!* I longed to proclaim such grace to the whole world of sinners.

Feb. 17, 1745. On the sunny side of a hill in the wilderness, I preached all day, to people who had come twenty miles to hear me, on *Jesus stood and cried, If any man thirst, let him come unto Me and drink!* I was scarce ever enabled to offer the free grace of God to perishing sinners with more plainness.

April 22, 1745. Preached, with freedom and life, from *Jesus stood and cried, If any man thirst, let him come unto Me and drink!*

August 5, 1745. Preached to the Indians from *Jesus stood and cried, If any man thirst, let him come unto Me and drink!* Some, who had never been affected before, were struck with deep concern; others had their concern greatly deepened.

He died on October 9, 1747. He was not yet thirty, but he had no regrets. 'Now that I am dying,' he exclaimed, 'I declare that I would not for all the world have spent my life otherwise!' Near the end, Miss Edwards, to whom he was betrothed, and who followed him into the unseen about four months later, entered the sickroom with a Bible in her hand. 'Oh, that dear book!' he cried, 'that lovely book! I shall soon see it opened! The mysteries in it, and the mysteries of God's providence, will all be unfolded!' Thus he clung to the promise of the text to the last. He was radiantly confident that the thirst of the soul—the thirst for knowledge and illumination—the thirst that had been only partially quenched in this world—would be abundantly satisfied in the realms of everlasting light.

3
SIR ERNEST SHACKLETON'S TEXT
1874–1922
British Antartic explorer and author.

Psalm 139:9–10

I

FLAME or frost; it makes no difference. A truth that, in one age, can hold its own in a burning fiery furnace can, in another, vindicate itself just as readily amidst fields of ice and snow.

'One, two, three—*four!*' counted the king, as he gazed in astonishment upon the Babylonian furnace.

'One, two, three—*four!*' exclaimed the explorer, in reverent delight, as he forced his hazardous way over the snowdrifts and glaciers of the terrible Antarctic.

'And Nebuchadnezzar the king was astonished, and rose up in haste, and spake, and said unto his counsellors, Did not we cast *three* men bound into the midst of the fire? They answered and said, True, O King! He answered and said, Lo, I see *four* men loose, walking in the midst of the fire, and they have no hurt, and *the form of the fourth is like the Son of God.*'

'We all felt that there were, not *three,* but *four* of us,' said Sir Ernest Shackleton. He was speaking at a banquet given in London in his honor, and was describing the thrilling adventures of the Rescue Expedition, as, after the sinking of the *Endurance,* they made their way in an open boat—a twenty-foot whaler—over eight hundred miles of stormswept sea, and then crawled and clambered over the dizzy peaks and slippery glaciers of South Georgia—the gate of the Antarctic—in order that they might obtain succor for their twenty comrades marooned on Elephant Island. As Sir Ernest told his story, the listeners held their breath. That lonely voyage on a polar sea, and that intrepid climb over uncharted ranges, was the wildest adventure of the speaker's life. Mr. Edward Marston, the well-known artist, accompanied Shackleton to the South, and was one of the men who owed their lives to that astounding journey. Mr. Marston declares that his leader's voyage in the open boat is one of the most magnificent feats of courage ever performed, whilst his climb across the frozen heights of South Georgia, never before accomplished by man, was one of splendid, almost incredible endurance. 'His repeated attempts to reach and rescue us,' Mr. Marston adds, 'and his ultimate success in the face of apparently insuperable difficulties, proved the indomitable perseverance of his mind.' At that London banquet Shackleton said nothing of these historic heroisms of his; but he said something no less notable. 'You could have heard a pin drop,' says one who was present, 'when Sir Ernest spoke of his consciousness of a Divine Companion in his journeyings.' Happily, the explorer afterwards wrote a book, and, in the stirring pages of *South,* he has left the story on imperishable record. 'When,' he says, 'I look back upon those days, with all their anxiety and peril, I cannot doubt that our party was divinely guided, both over the snowfields and across the stormswept sea. I know that, during that long and racking march of thirty-six hours over the unnamed mountains and glaciers of South Georgia, it seemed to me, very often, that we were, not *three*, but *four!* I said nothing to my companions on the point, but afterwards Worsley said to me: "Boss, I had a curious feeling on the march that there was *Another Person* with us." Crean confessed to the same idea. One feels the dearth of human words, the roughness of mortal speech in trying to tell of things intangible, but a record of our journeys would be incomplete without a reference to a subject very near our hearts.'

Shadrach, Meshach, Abednego and—*Another!*

Shackleton, Worsley, Crean and—*Another!*

One, two, three—*four,* in the fiery furnace!

One, two, three—*four,* in the stormy seas and in the frozen snow!

And lo, *the form of the fourth was like the Son of God!*

II

Having given us, both with his lips and with his pen, this noble testimony, Sir Ernest set himself to prepare for his last—and fatal—voyage. It was not his custom to take with him anything with which he could dispense; but he insisted on including among his treasures a gramophone record of Dame Clara Butt's rendering of *Abide with Me*. He wanted to be assured in that melodious way that the Invisible Companion of his former expedition would constantly attend him on this one. 'Just think,' said a London writer at the time, 'just think of those words and of that music—"I need Thy presence every passing hour"—ringing out across the icebound wastes of the Antarctic!' It was Shackleton's one thought, and it grew upon him towards the close. 'As we made that journey over the icy ranges,' he says, 'we saw God in His splendors and heard *the text that Nature renders.*' And what was the text? We are left in no uncertainty. Just before leaving England for the last time, he delivered an address, in the course of which he repeated his testimony concerning his Unseen Comrade. Miss Ada E. Warden, who was present, says that 'after repeating the story of the appalling voyage in the open boat from Elephant Island to South Georgia, he quoted the words from the one hundred and thirty-ninth Psalm: *"If I take the wings of the morning, and dwell in the uttermost parts of the sea, even there shall Thy hand lead me and Thy right hand shall hold me."* He repeated the words most impressively, and said that they were a continual source of strength to him. I, for one, shall never read those beautiful words without recalling his testimony.'

'We were comrades with Death all the time,' he

said to Mr. Harold Begbie in the course of a casual conversation, 'but I can honestly say that it wasn't bad. We always felt that there was Something Above. You know the words—*If I take the wings of the morning, and dwell in the uttermost parts of the sea, even there shall Thy hand lead me and Thy right hand shall hold me.* That Psalm exactly fitted our case.'

'*One, two three—four!*'

'*In life, in death, O Lord, abide with me!*'

'*If I take the wings of the morning, and dwell in the uttermost parts of the sea, even there shall Thy hand lead me and Thy right hand shall hold me.*'

There can, then, be no shadow of doubt about Sir Ernest Shackleton's text. His body has been laid to rest among the eternal snows, close to the scene of his most daring exploit. 'To another sea,' as Mr. Begbie says, 'he has now sailed his ship, a sea of silence, darkness and mystery, but with a coastline glowing in the rays of a brighter sun. Across that sea many greater spirits have sailed, but few, I think, with steadier hearts and eyes more eager for new shores.' He has bequeathed to us an example and a testimony that will live for evermore.

III

Yes, that text is Shackleton's text; but it is not Shackleton's alone. It is every traveller's text. It comforted Enoch Arden on the day on which he sailed; and, with it, he, in his blunt sailor-fashion, tried to comfort poor Annie:

'Annie, my girl, cheer up, be comforted,
Look to the babes, and, till I come again,
Keep everything ship-shape, for I must go.
And fear no more for me; or, if you fear,
Cast all your cares on God; that anchor holds!
Is He not yonder in those uttermost
Parts of the morning? if I flee to these
Can I go from Him? and the sea is His,
The sea is His: He made it.'

Before I settled at my present church I had the honor of holding two pastorates: one in New Zealand and one in Tasmania. In New Zealand no name is more honored than that of Bishop Selwyn; in Tasmania none is more cherished than that of Sir John Franklin. Now here is a striking and impressive coincidence! When young Selwyn landed in New Zealand, that country was the land of the Maori; and the Maori had the reputation of being the most ferocious of cannibals. The youthful Bishop looked around upon a land of volcanic wonders and of the most unusual vegetation. When Sunday came, he conducted his very first service in the new land. Turning for a moment from the natives to his white companions, he exclaimed: 'A great change has taken place in the circumstances of our natural life; but no change which need affect our spiritual being. We have come to a land where not so much as a tree resembles those of our native

country. All visible things are new and strange:
but the things that are unseen remain the same.'
And he took, as the text of that first sermon in
New Zealand, the text from which, nearly a century
later, Sir Ernest Shackleton drew such wealthy
stores of inspiration: *If I take the wings of the
morning, and dwell in the uttermost parts of the
sea, even there shall Thy hand lead me and Thy
right hand shall hold me.*

So much for Bishop Selwyn: now for Sir John
Franklin, whose statue I passed every day at Hobart.
Sir Francis Leopold McClintock, away in Arctic
seas, found a boat-load of bones, representing all
that remained of the Franklin expedition. And with
the bones were some Bibles. For some time these
Bibles were to be seen at the United Service Museum, and visitors were deeply impressed at the sight
of one in which these words had been marked and
underlined: *If I take the wings of the morning,
and dwell in the uttermost parts of the sea, even
there shall Thy hand lead me and Thy right hand
shall hold me.*

'Even there!' 'Even there!'
Out in the unknown—with Enoch Arden!
At the Antipodes—with Selwyn!
In the frozen North—with Franklin!
At the Antarctic—with Shackleton!
'Even there!' 'Even there!'
*Even there shall Thy hand lead me and Thy right
hand shall hold me.*

IV

In the development of Church history there have been scores of heresy hunts; but there have only been two heresies. Adam started the first, and Cain inaugurated the second. The first was the heresy of *Thereness*: the second was the heresy of *Hereness*. Adam believed that God was *there,* but not *here:* so he hid. Cain believed that God was *here,* but not *there;* so he went out from the presence of the Lord and dwelt in the land of Nod. The heretics of the Old Testament were all of them enslaved by one or other of these twin fallacies. Jacob, for example, thought of God as a poor little tribal deity who could lend Himself to trickery and cunning, and who dwelt in the narrow slice of land in which his father happened to reside. It came upon him as a bewildering surprise that, in his fugitive flight, he had not evaded the vigilant care of the Most High. From his stony pillow in the wilderness there was a ladder that led to heaven, and, wherever he fled, God's angels were! Naaman's pitiful conception of God led him to carry home with him two mules' burden of the soil of Canaan that he might enjoy the superstitious satisfaction of praying to Jehovah on the very soil that His Spirit pervaded. Jonah cherished the thought of a God who could readily be evaded by the simple expedient of crossing the sea. From the deck of a gallant vessel of Tarshish he waved a confident good-bye to the God whom he was leaving behind. The heresies of *Hereness* and *Thereness* have blighted ten thousand lives, and they may easily blight ours.

They almost wrecked the faith of Uncle Tom. Uncle Tom had been sold away from the old Kentucky home; and, herded with a throng of other slaves, was being carried on a steamboat up the Red River. All that he loved was left behind. That night he sat on the deck in the moonlight; and, for the first time, his faith staggered. It really seemed to him that, in leaving Aunt Chloe and the children and his old companions, he was leaving God! He could believe that God dwelt in old Kentucky; but how could God dwell among the horrors of the Red River? 'Is God *here?*' he asked himself, again and again; and, at last, disconsolate, he threw himself upon the floor and fell asleep. And, in his sleep, he dreamed. He dreamed that he was back again, and that little Eva was reading to him from the Bible as of old. He could hear her voice: *When thou passest through the waters, I will be with thee; for I am the Lord thy God, the Holy One of Israel, thy Saviour.* A little later, poor Tom was writhing under the cruel lash of his new owner. 'But,' says Mrs. Stowe, 'the blows fell only upon the outer man, and not, as before, on the heart. Tom stood submissive; and yet Legree could not hide from himself the fact that his power over his victim had gone. As Tom disappeared in his cabin, and Legree wheeled his horse suddenly round, there passed through the tyrant's mind one of those vivid flashes that often send the lightning of conscience across the dark and wicked soul. He understood full well that it was God who was standing between him and Tom, and he blasphemed Him!'

'*Is God here?*' Tom asked, that dreadful night.

'*When thou passest through the waters, I will be with thee,*' said the gentle little voice in the dream.

'*Legree knew that it was God who stood between his victim and himself.*'

For—'*even there, even there, shall Thy hand lead me and Thy right hand shall hold me.*'

Even there! Even there!

In his *Scapegoat,* Sir Hall Caine has very tenderly portrayed the hunger of the heart for the father's presence. Little Naomi is deaf and dumb and blind. Her mother is dead. She lives with her father, and he is an alien in a strange land. And often, in the night, Israel would wake and find the silent little figure, robed in white, standing beside his bed. Darkness and light were alike to her. She could not tell him why she came. She just wanted to feel that he was near. 'So, with a sigh, he would arise and light his lamp and lead her back to bed, and, more scalding than the tears that would be standing in Naomi's eyes, would be the hot drops that would gush into his own.'

The Unseen Comrade! The Invisible Companion! The Hunger of the Heart for the Father's

Presence! Livingstone felt it in the burning heat of Africa; Shackleton felt it amidst the blinding whiteness of the frozen South. *'Abide with me!'* he prayed. It was the child feeling, like little Naomi, for the father's hand. Did the words sing themselves to his soul at the last?

Be Thou Thyself before my closing eyes;
Shine through the gloom, and point me to the skies:
Heaven's morning breaks and earth's vain shadows flee;
In life—in death—O Lord, abide with me!

I do not know whether, as he set out on his last long journey, these favorite words of his came back to him. I only know—and he knew—that the Invisible Comrade was there. He never fails nor forsakes. *'If I take the wings of the morning, and dwell in the uttermost parts of the sea, even there shall Thy hand lead me and Thy right hand shall hold me.'* He has taken the wings of a new morning, but the old promise holds good. The Father will clasp the hand of His child on any sea and on any shore.

4

GEORGE WHITEFIELD'S TEXT
1714–1770
English evangelist to Great Britain and America.

John 3:3

I

GEORGE WHITEFIELD was the first man who treated Great Britain and America as if they both belonged to him. He passed from the one to the other as though they were a pair of rural villages, and he was the minister in charge of the parish. George Whitefield took a couple of continents under his wing; and the wing proved capacious enough for the task.

In days when the trip was a serious undertaking, he crossed the Atlantic thirteen times; but, of all his voyages, this was the worst. Day after day, ploughing her way through terrific seas, the good ship had shuddered in the grip of the gale. The sailors were at their wits' end: the sails were torn to ribbons and the tackling was all strained and broken. George Whitefield, who, wrapped in a buffalo hide, sleeps in the most protected part of the vessel, has been drenched through and through twice in one night. The ship has been so buffeted and beaten that nearly three months have passed before the Irish coast is sighted. Rations have been reduced to famine fare. The gravest anxiety marks every countenance.

To-day, however, there is a lull in the storm. The seas have moderated and the sun is shining. In the afternoon, Mr. Whitefield assembles the passengers and crew, and conducts a service on the deck. Have a good look at him! He is twenty-five, tall, graceful and well proportioned; of fair complexion and bright blue eyes. There is a singular cast in one of those eyes, which, though not unsightly, has the curious effect of making each hearer feel that the preacher is looking directly at him. There is something extraordinarily commanding about him; it was said that, by raising his hand, he could reduce an unruly rabble of twenty thousand people to instant silence. His voice, strong and rich and musical, was so perfectly modulated and controlled that his audiences were charmed into rapt attention. It had phenomenal carrying power. Whilst Whitefield was preaching in the open air one day, Benjamin Franklin, who was present, made a singular computation. He walked backwards until he reached a point at which he could no longer hear every word distinctly. He marked the spot and afterwards measured the distance. As a result, he calculated that Mr. Whitefield could command an audience of thirty thousand people without straining his voice in the least.

To-day, however, instead of thirty thousand people, he has barely thirty. Standing on the hatchway, with a coil of rope at his feet, he announces his text: *'Verily, verily, I say unto thee, Except a man be born again, he cannot see the kingdom of God.'* The passengers lounging about the deck, and the sailors leaning against the bulwarks, listen

breathlessly as, for half an hour, an earnest and
eloquent man pours out his heart in personal testimony, powerful exposition and passionate entreaty.
'Every man,' he cries, 'who has even the least concern for the salvation of his precious and immortal
soul should never cease watching and praying and
striving till he find a real, inward, saving change
wrought in his heart, and thereby doth know of a
truth that he has been *born again.*'

   *'Verily, verily, I say unto thee, Except a man be
born again, he cannot see the kingdom of God.'*
That is George Whitefield's text in mid-Atlantic because it is George Whitefield's text on both sides of
the Atlantic.   In season and out of season, in public
and in private, he ceaselessly proclaimed that message.   He felt that he was sent into the world to
call the attention of men to that one mandatory word.
He is known to have preached more than three
hundred times from this memorable and striking
passage.   And nobody who has read the story of
his spiritual travail will marvel for a moment at his
having done so.

II

   For it was that great text about *the new birth* that
had thrown open to him the gates of the kingdom of
God.   He was only a schoolboy when it first dawned
upon him that, between him and that kingdom, a
frightful chasm yawned.   'I got acquainted,' he says,
'with such a set of debauched, abandoned, atheistical

youths that if God, by His free grace, had not delivered me out of their hands, I should long ago have sat in the scorner's chair. I took pleasure in their lewd conversation. My thoughts of religion became more and more like theirs. I affected to look rakish and was in a fair way of being as infamous as the worst of them.' Then came the sudden arrest, the quick realization of his folly; and the vision of the hideous blackness of his own heart. But how to cure it? that was the problem. He resolved to change, at any rate, his *outward* bearing. 'As, once, I affected to look more rakish, so now I strove to appear more grave than I really was.' This, however, was cold comfort; it was like painting rotten wood: he was conscious all the time of the concealed corruption. He tried another course. He denied himself every luxury; wore ragged and even dirty clothes; ate no foods but those that were repugnant to him; fasted altogether twice a week; gave his money to the poor; and spent whole nights in prayer lying prostrate on the cold stones or the wet grass. But it was all of no avail. He felt that there was something radically wrong in the very heart of him, something that all this penance and self-degradation could not change. Then came the Angel of Deliverance; and the Angel of Deliverance bore three golden keys. One was a *man:* one was a *book:* one was a *text.*

The *man* was Charles Wesley, the minstrel of Methodism. George Whitefield and Charles Wesley were, by this time, fellow-students at Oxford. Wesley noticed the tall, grave youth, always walking alone, apparently in deep thought; and he felt strangely drawn to him. They met. Forty years afterwards Charles Wesley commemorated that meeting:

> Can I the memorable day forget,
> When first we by divine appointment met?
> Where undisturbed the thoughtful student roves,
> In search of truth, through academic groves;
> A modest pensive youth, who mused alone,
> Industrious the beaten path to shun,
> An Israelite, without disguise or art,
> I saw, I loved, and clasped him to my heart,
> A stranger as my bosom friend caressed,
> And unawares received an angel-guest!

But, if Whitefield was 'an angel-guest' to Charles Wesley, Charles Wesley was certainly no less to Whitefield. Whitefield often referred to him as 'my never-to-be-forgotten friend.' In those days Charles Wesley also was groping after the light: he could not, therefore, solve his new friend's aching problem: but he could lend him the books that he himself was reading; and he did.

The *book* that Charles Wesley lent George Whitefield was Henry Scougal's *The Life of God in the Soul of Man.* He read it with amazement and delight. It told him exactly what he longed to know. He learned for the first time that true religion is a union of the soul with God; it is Christ formed within us. 'When I read this,' he says, 'a ray of divine light instantaneously darted in upon my soul; and, from that moment, but not till then, did I know that I must become *a new creature.*' He is a young man of twenty-one. 'After having undergone innumerable buffetings by day and night, God was pleased at length,' he says, 'to remove my heavy load and to enable me, by a living faith, to lay hold on His dear Son. And oh! with what joy—joy unspeakable and full of glory—was I filled when the weight of sin left me and an abiding sense of the pardoning love of God broke in upon my disconsolate soul!' His first act in his ecstasy was to write to all his relatives. 'I have found,' he tells them, 'that there is such a thing as *the new birth.*'

'I must be a new creature!'

'There is such a thing as the new birth!'

'Verily, verily, I say unto thee, Except a man be born again, he cannot see the kingdom of God!'

It was thus that the *man* introduced the *book;* and the *book* introduced the *text;* and the *text* led George Whitefield into the kingdom of God. 'I know the exact place,' he says. 'It may perhaps be superstitious, but, whenever I go to Oxford, I cannot help running to the spot where Jesus Christ first revealed Himself to me and gave me *a new birth.*'

III

A new creature!
The new birth!

'Except a man be born again. . . .'

What does it mean? It means, if it means anything, that the miracle of Creation's morning may
be re-enacted: a man may be made all over again.
He may be changed root and branch: the very fibre
and fabric of his manhood may be transfigured.
You ask me to explain this *new* creation: I will do
so when you have explained the *earlier* one. You
ask me to explain this *second* birth: I merely re-
mind you that the *first* birth—the physical and intellectual one—is involved in inscrutable mystery.

I cannot explain the creation of the universe; but,
for all that, here is *the universe!*

I cannot explain the mystery of birth; but what
does it matter? here is *the child!*

I cannot explain the truth that, darting like a flash
of lightning into the soul of that Oxford student,
transforms his whole life; but, explained or unex-
plained, here is *George Whitefield!*

'O Lord,' muttered Alexander Pope one day,
'make me a *better* man!'

'It would be easier,' replied his spiritually-en-
lightened page, 'to make you a *new* man!'

And in that distinction lies the whole doctrine that
so startled and captivated and dominated the life of
George Whitefield.

IV

With this text burned into his very soul, and inscribed indelibly upon his mind, George Whitefield

mapped out the programme of his life. He set himself to a stupendous and world-wide campaign; he determined that he would carry that one message everywhere. He was forever on the march; and he was forever and ever proclaiming, with the most affecting fervor and persuasion, that *except a man be born again, he cannot see the kingdom of God.* David Garrick used to say that he would gladly give a hundred guineas to be able to pronounce the word 'Oh!' as movingly as Whitefield did. The secret was that all Whitefield's soul was in that yearning monosyllable. He was hungry for the salvation of men. He remembered his own bewilderment, his own frantic struggle for freedom; and he longed to shed upon others the light that had broken so startlingly and joyously upon him. He could scarcely speak of anything else. In preaching a funeral sermon soon after Mr. Whitefield's death, the Rev. Joseph Smith, V.D.M., said that 'there was scarcely one sermon in which Mr. Whitefield did not insist upon the necessity of *the new birth.* With passionate vehemency and earnest repetition he cried again and again: *'Verily, verily, I say unto thee, Except a man be born again, he cannot see the kingdom of God.'* He found that the hearts of men were waiting wistfully for that message.

He tells us, for example, of one of his earliest efforts. It was at Kingswood. He was refused permission to preach in the church unless he would undertake to say nothing about *the new birth.* But

that was the very subject on which he was determined to speak. He therefore resorted to the open
fields; and the miners, in their thousands, thronged
around him. 'I preached,' he says, 'on the Saviour's words to Nicodemus, *Ye must be born again;*
and the people heard me gladly. Having no righteousness of their own to renounce, they were delighted to hear of One who came not to call the
righteous but sinners to repentance. The first discovery of their being affected was to see the white
gutters made by the tears which streamed plentifully
down their black cheeks as they came fresh from
the coalpit. Hundreds and hundreds of them were
soon brought under deep convictions which happily
ended in sound and thorough conversion. The
change was visible to all.'

The news spread through the country that a cultured and eloquent preacher was declaring to great
multitudes on village greens, at street corners, at
fairs and fêtes, at festivals, on bowling greens and
in open fields that men might be remade, regen-
erated, *born again.* The inhabitants of towns that
he had not yet visited sent to him, begging him to
come. When, for example, he was approaching
Bristol, multitudes went out on foot to meet him;
and the people saluted and blessed him as he passed
along the street. The churches were so crowded that
it was with difficulty that he could obtain access to
the pulpit. Some hung upon the rails of the organ-
loft; others climbed upon the leads of the church; at

every crack and crevice ears were straining to catch the message. When he preached his last sermon in the town, and told the people that they would see his face no more, they all—high and low, young and old—burst into tears. Multitudes followed him to his rooms weeping; the next day he was employed from daylight till midnight in counselling eager inquirers; and, in the end, he left the town secretly at dead of night, in order to evade the throng that would have insisted on attending him.

V

George Whitefield made the doctrine of *the new birth* his universal message because he found that it met a universal need. I catch glimpses of him under many skies and under strangely varied conditions; but he is always proclaiming the same truth, and always with the same result.

Here he is, seated with an Indian in a canoe on one of the great American rivers! He is visiting the various encampments of the Delawares. He loves to go from tribe to tribe, and from wigwam to wigwam, telling the red men, by the aid of an interpreter, that a man of any kind and any color may be *born again.* For hundreds of miles, he trudges his way through the solitudes of the great American forests that he may deliver to Indians and backwoodsmen the message that is burning in his soul.

Here he is, preaching to the black men of Ber-

mudas! *'Except,'* he cries, *'except a man be born
again, he cannot see the kingdom of God.'* 'Attention,' he tells us, 'sat on every face. I believe there
were few dry eyes. Even the negroes who could
not get into the building, and who listened from
without, wept plentifully. Surely a great work is
begun here!'

Here he is in Scotland! He is visiting Cambus-
lang; and there is no building large enough to
accommodate any considerable fraction of the
crowds that throng to hear him. He therefore
preaches in the glen. The grassy level by the burn-
side, and the steep brae which rises from it in the
form of an amphitheatre, offer a noble and impressive auditorium. 'He dwelt mostly on *Regener-
ation,'* the record tells us. And the result vindicated
his choice of a theme. On the last Sunday of his
stay he preached to between thirty and forty
thousand people, whilst over three thousand par-
ticipated in the closing communion.

Here he is in the Countess of Huntingdon's
drawing-room! The sumptuous apartment is
thronged by princes and peers, philosophers and
poets, wits and statesmen. To this select and aristocratic assembly he twice or thrice every week
delivers his message. *'Ye must be born again!'* he
says; and he implores his titled hearers to seek the
regenerating grace that can alone bring the joy of
heaven into the experiences of earth.

Here he is, bending over his desk. He is writing

to Benjamin Franklin—'the man who wrenched the sceptre from tyrants and the lightning from heaven.' 'I find,' he says, 'that you grow more and more famous in the learned world. As you have made such progress in investigating the mysteries of electricity, I now humbly urge you to give diligent heed to the mystery of *the new birth*. It is a most important and interesting study, and, when mastered, will richly repay you for your pains.'

I could change the scene indefinitely. But in every country, and under every condition, he is always expatiating on one tremendous theme:

'Verily, verily, I say unto thee, Except a man be born again, he cannot see the kingdom of God.'

He cannot help it. When, at Oxford, he first discovered the necessity, and experienced the power, of *the new birth,* he could speak of nothing else. 'Whenever a fellow-student entered my room,' he says, 'I discussed with him our Lord's words about being *born again.'* For thirty years he preached night and day on the theme that had torn the shackles from his own soul. Towards the close of his *Life of George Whitefield,* Mr. J. P. Gledstone gives a list of the eminent preachers, poets and philanthropists who, together with countless thousands of less famous men, were led into the kingdom and service of Christ as a result of Mr. Whitefield's extraordinary ministry. He often said that he should like to die in the pulpit, or immediately after leaving it; and he almost had his wish. He preached the day before he died; and he remained true to his own distinctive message to the last. 'I am now fifty-five years of age,' he said, in one of these final addresses, 'and I tell you that I am more than ever convinced that the truth of *the new birth* is a revelation from God Himself, and that without it you can never be saved by Jesus Christ.'

'Why, Mr. Whitefield,' inquired a friend one day, 'why do you so often preach on *Ye must be born again?*'

'Because,' replied Mr. Whitefield, solemnly, looking full into the face of his questioner, 'because *ye must be born again!*'

That is conclusive. It leaves nothing more to be said!

5

CARDINAL NEWMAN'S TEXT
1801–1890
Anglican clergyman and later Roman Catholic cardinal.

Isaiah 53

I

BY some strange witchery peculiar to himself, John
Henry Newman contrived to interest a whole nation
in his own spiritual history. No man ever succeeded as did he in making his soul's secret struggle
a matter of general conversation and popular excitement. It is difficult, at this distance of time, to
understand the irresistible appeal that he made to
the universal imagination, and the indisputable
authority that he wielded over the public mind. For
years his word counted for more than that of any
other teacher: he was quite easily the greatest religious genius of his time. For one thing, everybody seemed to know him: his very appearance
was striking, magnetic, compelling. Anthony
Froude, who knew him well, tells us that he was
above the middle height, slight and spare. 'His
head was massive, his face remarkably like that of
Julius Cæsar. The forehead, the shape of the ears
and nose as well as the lines of the mouth, were all
peculiar, and I should say, exactly like Cæsar's. I
have often thought of the resemblance and believe
that it extended to the temperament. For he was

imperious and wilful, although, along with these traits, his character was marked by a most engaging gentleness, sweetness and singleness of purpose.' Even down to extreme old age, Mr. Froude says, he attracted and retained the passionate devotion of his friends and followers.

His early history was familiar to every Englishman. His wistful and pathetic pilgrimage—and especially the pilgrimage that enriched our literature by the addition of *Lead, Kindly Light*—had been followed with breathless curiosity and deepening compassion. And when, at length, he retired to Littlemore to settle the question on which everything depended, an entire people waited for his decision with the strained intensity with which, at other times, they await the result of a General Election or the issue of an important military engagement. In that modest cottage at Littlemore, the lonely thinker—shut up to his vigils and fastings and prayers—appeared to the multitude as a kind of intellectual Crusoe. Cut off from everything and everybody, he seemed the emblem of utter isolation. Men wondered whether deliverance would come to him, and, if so, how and when. The whole world knows how that grim struggle ended. 'My dearest Pusey,' he writes, in a letter that has become historic, and that bears the date October 8, 1845, 'this will not go till all is over. This night I am expecting Father Dominic, the Passionist. I trust he will receive me into what I believe to be the one and only

Fold of the Redeemer. I do not expect it will take place before Friday.'

When the silver was creeping into his hair, Robinson Crusoe revisited his island. When Newman was an old man, withered, and bent—perhaps also brokenhearted and disappointed—he paid a secret pilgrimage to Littlemore. He endeavored to evade recognition, but the curate of the little place detected him. Mr. Lytton Strachey tells the touching story. 'As,' he says, 'the curate was passing by the church, he noticed an old man, very poorly dressed in an old grey coat, with the collar turned up, leaning over the lych-gate, in floods of tears. He was apparently in great trouble, and his hat was pulled down over his eyes, as if he wished to hide his features. For a moment, however, he turned towards the curate, who was suddenly struck by something familiar in the face. Could it be——? A photograph hung over the curate's mantelpiece of the man who had made Littlemore famous by his memorable sojourn there; he had never seen the original; but now, was it possible——? He looked again, and he could doubt no longer. It was Dr. Newman! He sprang forward with proffers of assistance. Could he be of any use? "Oh, no, no!" was the reply. "Oh, no, no!" But the curate felt that he could not turn away and leave so eminent a character in such distress. "Was it not Dr. Newman he had the honor of addressing?" he asked, with all the respect and sympathy at his command.

"Was there nothing that could be done?" But the old man hardly seemed to understand what was being said to him. "Oh, no, no!" he repeated, with the tears streaming down his face. "Oh, no, no!" '

It was not until many years after the crisis had passed that the story of that silent struggle at Littlemore was fully told. The letter to Pusey was written in 1845: the *Apologia pro Vita Sua* was published in 1864. Yet the interest of the people had not waned. Although he warned the nation that he had no romantic story to tell, the multitudes waited for his confessions with the avidity with which men await the thrilling narrative of a polar explorer. 'Not the *Letters* of Pascal,' says Dr. William Barry, 'nor those of Junius, won more instant success. The *Apologia* appeared in all hands, was read in clubs, in drawing-rooms, at street corners, on the tops of omnibuses, and in railway trains; and everywhere the person of the author was discussed and his pathetic and striking sentences quoted.' And why? Dr. Barry gives the reason. 'Here,' he says, 'instead of a fresh volume added to the interminable stores of controversy, was a life, revealed in its innermost workings, *the heart put under a glass that made it transparent*. It had been Rousseau's boast that he would do this unparalleled thing; he would reveal his secret soul; and he did it—at what a cost to the decencies of human reticence, to the laws of friendship, to the claims of gratitude! Newman, observing a punctilious self-respect, nor making free with any other man's reputation, set up in the Temple of Fame this tablet, on which all might read the story of his days, anticipating, said Mr. Gladstone, whom it awed and overcame, the last great Judgment itself.'

Here, then, is Cardinal Newman, one of the strangest and saddest figures in our history! To the end of his days he was a child of the twilight. The *'encircling gloom'* was ever about him: he was always *'far from home.'* He was, it has been truly said, a pilgrim of eternity; but he was a pilgrim making his way *'o'er moor and fen, o'er crag and torrent till the night is gone.'* He was never at home in Protestantism; and the Church in whose lap he pillowed his throbbing brows left his heart still hungry. Yet, through the intervening mists, he saw far off the white glimmer of sunshine; through *the encircling gloom* he dimly beheld *the Kindly Light.* What was it? We shall see.

II

I was talking one day to an old ministerial friend —the Rev. Charles Bright, of South Australia— who told me a story concerning Newman, which, so far as I can discover, has never been printed before. Mr. Bright was, many years ago, a minister at Birmingham; and, in those days, Cardinal Newman was in residence at the Oratory at Edgbaston, near by. Mr. Bright was one evening spending an hour with a brother-minister named Walters, who, with his wife, had been holiday-making in South Wales. In the course of their tour, Mr. and Mrs. Walters stayed at Llandudno; and the landlady at whose house they engaged rooms, on discovering that they came from Birmingham, told them that, among her boarders, she had a Mr. Charles Newman, whose brother was a celebrated Roman Catholic priest in the city from which they had just come. Charles Newman was a poor fellow of feeble health, wandering intellect and grotesque hallucinations. He was for many years the anxiety and the burden of his celebrated brother.

'But,' continued Mr. Walters, 'the woman told us that she had a letter from the priest at Birmingham, and also a letter from another brother—Professor F. W. Newman—who lived at Bath. I asked her if she would mind showing me these letters. She said that she would be delighted, and seemed gratified at my interest. The letter from John Henry Newman, the priest, revealed deep concern for the welfare of his frail brother, and requested her to be sure to supply him with all that he required in the way of comfort and nourishment. He begged her, further, to bring the subject of Christianity as earnestly as possible under his brother's notice. If, he said, there was a Roman Catholic priest in or near Llandudno, he would like his brother to be visited by him. If, however, no priest was available, or if his brother should object to seeing such a priest, she was to do her best to induce him to receive the ministrations of a clergyman of the Church of England. Should the invalid refuse to see even an Anglican clergyman, she was *herself* to bring the deep need of his empty soul home to him in the best way known to her. *"And whatever else you do, or fail to do,"* added the priest at Edgbaston, *"you are to be sure to read to him the fifty-third chapter of the prophecy of Isaiah."* The letter from F. W. Newman simply urged her to secure for his brother every comfort and attention. I asked her,' continued Mr. Walters, 'if the letters were of any use to her. She saw my meaning at once, and said that "if I cared to have them, I was very welcome." '

'Mr. Walters brought the letters away with him,' Mr. Bright told me, 'and he pasted them in a book. And, during the evening that I spent at his house, he produced them and showed them to me.'

III

'Whatever else you do, or fail to do,' says the Cardinal, *'you are to be sure to read to him the fifty-third chapter of the prophecy of Isaiah.'*

The fifty-third of Isaiah! I can see the good landlady sitting in the room of her afflicted boarder, and from the Bible she reads to him the great words that his eminent brother has prescribed. Listen!

He was despised and rejected of men; a Man of Sorrows and acquainted with grief; and we hid as it were our faces from Him; He was despised and we esteemed Him not.

Surely He hath borne our griefs and carried our sorrows; yet we did esteem Him stricken, smitten of God and afflicted.

But He was wounded for our transgressions; He was bruised for our iniquities; the chastisement of our peace was upon Him, and with His stripes we are healed.

All we like sheep have gone astray; we have turned every one to his own way; and the Lord hath laid on Him the iniquity of us all.

'Whatever else you do, or fail to do, you are to be sure to read to him *the fifty-third of Isaiah.*' That *insistence* upon *the fifty-third of Isaiah* convinces me that, through *the encircling gloom,* Newman fixed his tired eyes upon the *Kindly Light.* Beyond the controversies and obscurities of Protestantism and Romanism, he saw *the Man of Sorrows, despised and rejected and acquainted with grief.*

IV

'The fifty-third chapter of Isaiah,' said Pusey, to whom that famous letter from Littlemore was written, 'the fifty-third chapter of Isaiah is *an antidote to the bitterness of any sorrow.*'

The Ethiopian eunuch thought so. He was compassed about by the *sorrows of Ignorance.* 'How can I understand,' he cried, 'except some man teach me?' And Philip stepped up into his chariot and expounded to him *the fifty-third of Isaiah!* 'Of whom speaketh the prophet this? of himself or of some other man?' asked the perplexed eunuch, as he read of *the Man of Sorrows, despised and rejected.* 'And Philip began at that same Scripture and preached unto him *Jesus.*' And, as a result, the eunuch went on his way rejoicing! The *fifty-third of Isaiah* had proved, as Dr. Pusey says, the antidote to the bitterness of his sorrow.

The Earl of Rochester thought so. He was plunged in the *sorrows of Scepticism.* Macaulay, in his *History of England,* speaks of Rochester's reclamation from atheism as one of the most signal triumphs of Bishop Gilbert Burnet. Yet the Bishop only did for the Earl what the evangelist did for the eunuch. He expounded to him *the fifty-third of Isaiah.* 'The Earl avowed, in pale astonishment, that the verses contained an accurate account of the life, character, trial, death and resurrection of the crucified Saviour. He thought it as plain as the history of Him given in the gospels.'

John Coleridge Patteson thought so; and, because he thought so, he devoted himself to his missionary life and died his martyr death. He was oppressed by the *sorrows of Sin.* As a little boy, he said that he should like to be a clergyman, because he thought that saying the Absolution to people must make them very happy. His first sermon, he used to tell his mother, should be on *the fifty-third of Isaiah.* He felt, as Pusey felt, that it would be the best antidote to the bitterness of sin's sorrows.

Philip Melancthon thought so. His heart was

heavy with the *sorrows of Farewell.* The frailty
of his body was compelling him to abandon his
work. On the last Good Friday of his life, he went
down to the University at Wittenberg and delivered
his final address. And he chose as his theme *the
fifty-third of Isaiah!*

John Knox thought so. He was encircled by the
sorrows of Death. And, during that last illness, he
asked that *the fifty-third of Isaiah* should be read
to him every day.

'Whatever else you do or fail to do,' says Newman, the writer of that letter from Littlemore, 'you
are to be sure to read to him *the fifty-third chapter
of the prophecy of Isaiah.*'

'For *the fifty-third chapter of Isaiah,*' says Pusey,
to whom that letter from Littlemore was addressed,
'is an antidote to the bitterness of any sorrow.'

But why? Why is Newman so anxious that *the
fifty-third of Isaiah* should be read to his brother?
And why is Pusey so sure that *the fifty-third of
Isaiah* is an antidote to the bitterness of any sorrow?
It is Bunyan's Greatheart who has given us the most
satisfying answer to these questions.

The pilgrims had enjoyed to the full the boun-
teous hospitality of good Mr. Gaius; and, before
taking leave of him, they brought their felicity to a
climax by joining in family worship. Christiana
asked her son James to read a chapter, so he read
the fifty-third of Isaiah. When he had finished, Mr.
Honest asked why it was said of the Saviour that

'*He had no form nor comeliness.*' 'The words are spoken,' replied Mr. Greatheart, 'concerning those who lack *the eye that can see into our Prince's heart.*'

That is very striking. Newman's biographer has told us that, by means of his *Apologia,* the Cardinal puts his heart under a microscope, so that every man can read it through and through. *The fifty-third of Isaiah* does for Newman's Saviour what the *Apologia* does for Newman. It enables us to peer into our Prince's very heart.

V

I have only heard of one person, in all the ages, to whose stricken soul *the fifty-third of Isaiah* brought no comfort at all; and that exception was a woman. For her *the fifty-third of Isaiah* gleamed with no Kindly Light: it was black with the darkness of midnight. *The fifty-third of Isaiah* was no antidote to the bitterness of *her* sorrow: it was sorrow's crown of sorrow. Mary, the mother of Jesus, it is said, could never bear to read *the fifty-third of Isaiah* herself, and she would never let her Divine Son read it. It was like a knife in her heart whenever she caught sight of the sublime passage. But the reason that made it as bitter as wormwood to her is the reason that has made it, to us, the fountain of all consolation and grace. For it was to *her* what it is to *us*—a glimpse into the heart that was to be broken at last upon the bitter Cross.

6

MARK SABRE'S TEXT

Character in A.S.M. Hutchinson's story *If Winter Comes.*

1 John 4:16

I

MARK SABRE wanted something. He could not tell anybody what it was that he wanted, for he did not know. He only knew that he carried in his heart a ceaseless hunger, an indescribable craving, an aching void. It is Mr. A. S. M. Hutchinson who, in *If Winter Comes,* tells his story; and that is how Mr. Hutchinson summarises his hero's spiritual destitution. And, in so summarising it, he displays a penetrating and practical insight. Here and there, as we go through life, we meet with a man who groans beneath a load of guilt; he feels, like Bunyan's pilgrim, that his burden is heavier than he can bear; and he longs for deliverance. He wants to *get rid of something.* But, for each such case, we meet with a dozen who are vaguely conscious that life is lacking; they are ashamed of their inner poverty; they think wistfully of the treasure in which others exult; they grope blindly but eagerly for that for which they would gladly sacrifice every penny they possess. They feel that they *need something.* So was it with Mark Sabre.

'We are all plugging about like mad because we are all *looking for something!*' he said to himself one morning, as he leaned back in his office chair, and yielded himself to his reflections. 'We are all *looking for something*. You can read it in half the faces you see. Some wanting—and knowing they are wanting—*something*. Others wanting *something*, but just putting up with it; content to be discontented. You can see it. And what is it that they are all looking for? It's some universal thing that's wanting—something that religion ought to give, but doesn't!'

Here then is the problem, or, rather, here are the two problems. The first is Browning's problem:

> Wanting is——what?
> Summer redundant.
> Blueness abundant——
> Where is the blot?

Mark Sabre feels that, for lack of that mysterious *something* whatever that *something* may be, life has become confused, involved, tangled, out of control. There are three women in the story, Mabel, Nona and Effie. He is married to Mabel. They have nothing in common; they do not seriously attempt to understand each other; no love is lost between them. He is whole-heartedly in love with Nona, and she with him; but Nona is the wife of Lord Tybar. Mark is determined that, come what may, his love for Nona shall never degrade or dishonor her. If he cannot help her upward, he will never drag her downward. He is resolved to play the game. But

the struggle is terrific. And he feels that, if only
that elusive and mysterious *something* had come into
his life at the start, this hideous complication would
have been averted. Life would have been under the
sway of a master-principle. Even now, if he could
but welcome that *something* into his heart, he might
be saved from shipwreck. He throws himself back
in his chair and reviews the situation.

Wanting is—what?—that is the *first* problem.
And, when he has discovered what he needs, whence
shall he obtain it?—that is the *second*.

II

Mark Sabre sought that evasive *something* in two
directions; but he found abiding satisfaction in
neither.

It occurred to him that *Friendship* is one of the
purest joys of life. He noticed that the hungry look
that he saw in people's eyes vanished when they
opened their hearts in confident, congenial communion with each other. It was so in his own case.
'How very glad his friends were to see him! It
was as though he brought them something—something very pleasurable to them and that they much
wanted. Certainly he, for his own part, received
such from them: a sense of warmth, a kindling of
the spirit, a glowing of all his affections and per-
ceptions. His mind would explore curiously this
train of thought. He came to determine that in-
finitely the most beautiful thing in life was a face

lighting up with the pleasure of friendship.' He remembered that *wanting something* look in the faces of half the people he saw; and he fancied that, by the rapture of friendship, even the weariest and most wistful faces were transfigured.

This was a hint: but only a hint. It did not carry him far. On reflection 'he felt that it was not entirely the secret. The friendly greeting passed: the light faded from the face: the wanting returned. The thing lacking was something that would fix it, render it permanent, establish it in the being as the heart is rooted in the body. *Something?* What?' This leads him to his second venture.

He wonders if it is *Faith* that he requires. 'Why is it,' he asks himself, 'that children's faces are always happy? There's something they must lose as they grow out of childhood. It's not that cares and troubles *come:* it is that something is *lost.* Well, what had I as a child that I have not as a man? Would it be hope? Would it be faith? Would it be belief?' Or are these three the same? It sets him thinking. He turns to the Churches; but, somehow, the Churches fail to satisfy him. He takes his friend, Hapgood, into his confidence.

'I tell you, Hapgood,' he says, 'that plumb down in the crypt and abyss of every man's soul is a hunger, a craving for other food than any earthly stuff. And the Churches know it; but instead of reaching down to him what he wants—light, light—instead of *that* they invite him to dancing and pic-

ture shows, and you're a jolly good fellow, and religion's a jolly fine thing and no spoil-sport, and all
that sort of latter-day tendency. Why, man, he can
get all that outside the Churches, and get it better.
Light, light! He wants light, Hapgood. And the
padres come down and drink beer with him, and
dance jazz with him, and call it making religion a
Living Thing in the Lives of the People. Lift the
hearts of the people to God, they say, by showing
them that religion is not incompatible with having
a jolly fine time. *And there's no God there that
a man can understand for him to be lifted to.* Hapgood, a man wouldn't care *what* he had to give up
if he knew he was making for something inestim-
ably precious. But he doesn't know. Light, light
—that's what he wants; and the longer it's withheld,
the lower he'll sink. Light! Light!'

And so *Society* fails him! And *the Churches* fail
him! And all the while the hunger of his heart for
that mysterious *something*—the *something* that he
feels he lacks—is growing. And all the while the
struggle becomes more fierce and terrible. Everything goes wrong at the office. Everything goes
wrong at home. The sympathies of life weaken:
the temptations of life strengthen: and still he is
without that *something* that would transform a
nebulous Chaos into an orderly Creation.

III

The great discovery, as he called it, broke suddenly upon him. The first hint of it came from Effie. Effie was a simple-hearted girl for whom he had obtained a situation as companion to an old lady whose son had gone to the war. Effie, Mr. Hutchinson tells us, was always 'happy. Nothing of that *wanting-something* look was ever to be seen in Effie's shining eyes; she had the secret of life. Watching her face while they talked, Sabre came to believe that the secret, the thing missing in half the faces he saw, was *love;* but—the old difficulty— many had love and yet were troubled. One evening he asked Effie a most extraordinary question, shot out of him without intending it; discharged out of his questioning thoughts as by a hidden spring suddenly touched by groping fingers.

'Effie, do you love God?'

'Why, of course I do, Mr. Sabre,' Effie answered in surprise.

'*Why* do you?'

She was utterly at a loss. 'Of course I do!' she said again.

'Yes,' he replied rather sharply, 'but *why?* Have you ever asked yourself *why?* Respecting, fearing, trusting; *that's* understandable. But *love!* You know what *love* is, don't you? What's *love* got to do with *God?*'

In simple wonderment, as though she had been asked what had the sun to do with light, or whether water was wet, she answered, 'Why, God *is* love!'

He stared at her. It was the first ray of clear sunshine that had broken upon him; and it startled him.

The grey dawn soon ripened into golden daylight. In the crisis of his career, when an avalanche of tragedies was overwhelming him, he again opened his heart to Hapgood.

'Hapgood,' he exclaimed, his face flushed with excitement, 'I've got the secret! I've got the key to the riddle that's been puzzling me all my life. I've got the new revelation in terms good enough for me to understand! I've got the light! Here it is: God is—*love!* Not this, that, nor the other that the intelligence revolts at, and puts aside, and goes away, and goes on hungering, hungering and unsatisfied; nothing like that; but just this: plain for a child, clear as daylight for grown intelligence: God is—*love!* Listen to this, Hapgood: *He that dwelleth in love, dwelleth in God and God in him; for God is love!* Isn't that a revelation? It explains everything to me. I can reduce all the mysteries to terms of *that.*'

And Hapgood tells us that through all the desperate days that followed—days of blackness impenetrable and of anguish unutterable—Sabre held on to that. 'He'd got this great discovery of his. Badly down as he was, at least he'd got *that!*'

'*He that dwelleth in love, dwelleth in God and God in him; for God is love*': that is Mark Sabre's text.

IV

I am not surprised. It is an exquisite phrase. *He that dwelleth in love*—that builds his nest *in love*—that makes his home *in love!* Let me call a pair of witnesses—Samuel Rutherford and Dr. Jowett.

'He that dwelleth in love, dwelleth in God.' 'O Sir,' exclaims Samuel Rutherford, writing to Colonel Ker in 1653, 'O Sir, what a house that must be! What is it to dwell *in love*—to live *in God?* How far are some from this, their house and home! How ill acquaint with the rooms, mansions, safety and sweetness of holy security to be found in God! When shall we attain to living *in Him* only—dwelling *in love;* residing *in God?'*

'He that dwelleth in love, dwelleth in God.' 'What a home!' exclaims Dr. J. H. Jowett. 'This home of the soul surpasses anything and everything for its loveliness and grace. *Dwelleth in love! Dwelleth in God!* There is nothing in nature which will provide an analogy gracious enough to carry the treasure. The soul which dwells in love radiates love. It looks out of its windows and has a feast of loveliness. It has a wonderful magic, and even deformed things begin to be transformed. If you would understand this magic and experience, change your address, and take up your home in *love,* for *he that dwelleth in love dwelleth in God, for God is love!'*

The whole point of Mr. Hutchinson's book is that

Mark Sabre actually entered into this celestial experience. He took up his residence in the love of God and caught the atmosphere of that divine dwelling-place.

V

I have said that everything went wrong with Sabre *at the office* and *at home*. Calamity followed hard upon the heels of calamity: tragedy after tragedy came thundering down upon him. *Somebody* had committed a great and terrible sin: *somebody* had driven poor Effie to a dreadful crime. Who was that *somebody?* With cruel unanimity, all the circumstances pointed to Sabre as the culprit; and, on the strength of that avalanche of evidence, Mabel had no difficulty in divorcing him.

At the office, there was a man whose heart extended its hospitality to a pitiless hate and a passionate love. It is wonderful how often those two opposites dwell together. Twyning, a partner in the firm, hated Sabre with a hate that was as cruel as death; and he loved his own boy—Harold Twyning—with an affection that was almost idolatry. Harold enlisted and went to the war. Whilst he was away in France, his father—not knowing that Sabre had offered for service and been rejected—kept up a running fire of biting sarcasms and sneering insinuations. And, mixing his love with his hate, he would mutter to himself in between whiles: 'My Harold! My Harold! Nobody knows what

Harold is to me! He's all the world to me; my boy, my boy! He's a better man than his father, a far better man! He's a good Christian, is Harold! He's never had a bad thought or said a bad word! My Harold! My Harold!'

VI

Then comes the sensation that forms the climax of the book. In the back of the clock—a place in which Effie used often to secrete things—Sabre finds a letter. It is addressed to him, and establishes his innocence completely! The guilty *somebody* was Harold Twyning! Harold was the father of Effie's child. The evidence in the divorce case was a tissue of false assumptions. It was Harold who had driven poor Effie to the murder of her babe and to suicide.

Sabre reads the letter again and again. He thinks of the stinging sarcasms to which he has been exposed at the office. He rises and mimics Twyning. 'Harold's such a good boy—never said a bad word or had a bad thought—such a good Christian model boy!' He determines to rush off to the office and show the letter to Twyning at once. 'He's hounded me to hell,' he says: 'at the very gates of hell, I've got him: I'll cram the letter down his throat!' His enemy, he feels, has been delivered into his hands!

He bursts into the office. Twyning sits at his desk, his head buried in his hands. At his elbows, vivid upon the black expanse of the table, lies a torn envelope, dull red.

'Twyning,' he begins, 'I've come to speak to you about your son!'

'Oh, Sabre; so you've heard! It was good of you to come, Sabre; I feel it! He's killed! My Harold! My boy! my boy, Harold! Oh, Sabre, such a good Christian boy! And he's gone; he's gone! Never to see him again; never again!' He began to sob. His head fell once more upon his hands; and Sabre strolled across to the fireplace. He was crumpling the letter in his hands. Stooping down, he held it over the flames—the letter that, of all things, alone declared his innocence. *With* that letter he could look the whole world in the face and hurl his worst enemies to confusion. *Without* that letter he stood convicted and condemned in the sight of all men. He remembered his text:

He that dwelleth in love, dwelleth in God, and God in him; for God is love.

'He opened his fingers,' Mr. Hutchinson says, 'and the crumpled letter was consumed. He went over and patted Twyning's heaving shoulders: "There, there, Twyning; bear up; bear up! Soldier's death! Fine boy! Died for his country! Bad luck, Twyning!" Twyning clutched his hand and squeezed it convulsively.' They parted, and Sabre went out to face the scowls of society.

Meanwhile, Nona, too, had been chastened by suffering and purified by trial. Her husband, whom she had come whole-heartedly to admire, had won the Victoria Cross and fallen at the front. When all the world turned its back upon Mark Sabre, she believed in him. She came to him at last; and, together, they entered into a felicity that they could never have known but for the temptations that they had resisted and the sufferings they had endured.

VII

Mark Sabre is not a perfect character. He is tactless, stupid, awkward. He has a genius for blundering. But, once he comes within the ambit of the love of God, his personality is irradiated and transfigured.

'Love . . . God . . . the love of God . . . God is love!' Did not the love of God reach its climax when He, the just, died for us, the unjust? He who knew no sin became the Lamb of God, bearing away the sins of the world. The innocent suffered for the guilty. So was it with Mark Sabre. When Sabre made his home in the love of God he became infected by the sacrificial spirit and fragrant atmosphere of that sublime abode.

7

ROBERT LAMB'S TEXT

d. about 1900 at age 45
Medical missionary to the Australian outback.

Matthew 11:28–30

I

ROBERT LAMB was a very gallant gentleman; and a
very gallant *Australian* gentleman at that. In order
that death might not deprive him of the privilege of
repeating his text—the text that he had expounded
with such delight, first to the savages of the South
Seas, and then to the swagmen of Australia—he
designed his own tombstone. That tombstone of his
is a thing of beauty and a joy forever. It is one of
the most eloquent and one of the most pathetic monuments to be found in the southern hemisphere. It
stands at the corner of a tiny bush burying-place,
tucked away among the giant mountains of New
South Wales; yet, by means of that roadside memo-
rial, Robert Lamb goes on repeating his text every
day of his deathless life. 'It is,' as Mr. J. A. Packer
says, 'a typical bush cemetery, overrun with weeds
and heather, as though no man or woman, much less
a sexton, ever gave it a thought. Few visitors to
the district go out of their way to inspect it; fewer
still of the many tourists who flash by in motor-
cars give it a second glance. Yet, hidden away here
in the heart of the mountains, swept by the westerly
winds, curtained by the enveloping mists, and wept

over by the rain-drops from the overarching gum
trees, is the resting-place of one of the greatest and
best men that this new land has known.'

If, *fifty* years before this bush burial took place,
you had stood on the spot that the monument now
occupies, you would have seen a pair of tired and
travel-stained pilgrims trudging wearily along the
dusty road. They are a young man and woman,
husband and wife. They are built of that stout stuff
of which the pioneers are always made. They have
ambitions, these two, but their dreams are based on
their willingness to suffer and to toil. Their swags
are strapped to their shoulders. Attracted by the
stories they have heard of the opening of new agri-
cultural areas in New Zealand, they have made up
their minds to try their fortunes there. The day of
railway trains has not yet dawned: there is nothing
for it but to trudge their way over mountain and
plain to the ship that will soon be sailing from Sydney. But the road seems interminable. They turn
the bend where the tomb now stands and begin to
climb the hill. Did no strange surge of unaccount-
able emotion sweep over them, I wonder, as they
glanced at that grassy plot beside the road? Did
the woman catch her breath? Did the man's heart,
just for a moment, seem to stand still? For they
reached New Zealand, these two, and prospered
there. There, too, a little boy was born to them.
And, fifty years after they dragged their blistered
feet along this endless road, that son of theirs—

greatly beloved and held in the highest honor—came
to these rugged mountains to ask of them a grave.
And, as his pitiless disease wore him down, his
thoughts flew back, almost hourly, to those two
brave pilgrims who, a few years before his birth,
had sanctified this dusty road for him by tramping
along it in the course of their great and gallant
venture. The vision suggested to him the beautiful
ministry by which his sunset days were adorned;
and it suggested to him the means by which he might
go on for centuries repeating to every wayfarer
his *text*.

II

If, *five* years before that bush burial took place,
you had stood on the spot that the monument now
occupies, you would have seen two men, engaged in
earnest conversation, sitting on a log by the side of
the road. The log is there still: a photograph of it
lies before me as I write. One of the men is a swagman, his swag is strapped to his shoulders; his billy
stands against the tuft of grass at his feet. He is an
arresting and picturesque figure; yet it is not to him,
but to his companion, that I wish to direct particular attention. For this is Dr. Robert Lamb; M.A.
of the University of New Zealand; M.B., Ch.M.,
and B.D. of the University of Edinburgh; one of
the most cultured, one of the most modest, and one
of the most lovable of men. Look at him! Although his consumption is beginning to play havoc

with his handsome form, he is still tall, well-knit and finely-proportioned. 'His face, with its well-trimmed black beard, wore a most beautiful expression,' writes one who knew him well. 'He had earnest hazel eyes, clear and kind, in which a fondness for fun seemed to be perpetually lurking. His forehead was lofty, giving an impression of immense intellectual resources. He was quiet and unobtrusive; his voice soft and persuasive; his step quick, his figure alert, and he himself the essence of gentleness, geniality and good temper.' This, then, is Robert Lamb. What of his story? And his *text?*

III

His story is soon told. The New Zealand farmer's boy—the son of those two travel-worn wayfarers that we saw vanishing over the crest of the hill—early displayed a restless curiosity and an insatiable thirst for knowledge. In studying for his degree he often wondered what he should do with the learning that he was so toilfully acquiring and with the powers that he was developing in the process. Then, one evening, at a great meeting held in St. Paul's Presbyterian Church, Christchurch, New Zealand— a church that I know well—he heard the Rev. Joseph Copeland plead for men who, at any hazard, would devote their lives to the evangelization of the New Hebrides. Mr. Copeland stirred the boy's fancy, fired his enthusiasm, and awoke in his heart a passionate desire to carry the message of light and life to the untutored barbarians who sat in darkness and in the shadow of death. His resolve lent new zest and significance to all his studies. He went on to Edinburgh; took the divinity and medical courses simultaneously; and, overtaxing his brilliant powers, paved the way for the malady that hurried him to an early grave.

He was nearly thirty when at last he reached the islands. He was appointed to Ambrym, a position of special peril. The natives had an ugly record; but Robert Lamb embraced the opportunity with unbounded delight. It really seemed, however, as if, from the very moment of his arrival, all things were conspiring to bring about his discomfiture and overthrow. 'I was privileged to be in close touch with him in those days,' says the Rev. A. J. Fraser. 'What his trials and sorrows were are known to few; but those few will always remember through what a fiery furnace Robert Lamb passed, and how the nobility of his character shone through it all.' Fever distressed him terribly from the very outset. 'There is so much to be done,' he writes, 'and I must go on as long as my poor legs can trot my hot cranium round!' He drove away his worries with a merry laugh; but, like a pack of hungry wolves, they crept stealthily back upon him. Sickness followed sickness, and trouble trod upon the heels of trouble, until, in March, 1893, the culminating calamity swooped down upon him. A frightful hurricane devastated the island; the mission station was completely wrecked; and his twin boys—Castor and Pollux, as he playfully called them—were killed. He bore his anguish bravely. With a smiling face he breasted the blows of circumstance and worked night and day to repair the pitiful havoc that the storm had wrought. He won the hearts of natives and missionaries alike. Many a time he rose from his own sick-bed at dead of night to tend and alleviate another's pain. 'By black men and by white,' says Dr. Marden, 'Robert Lamb was greatly beloved. Few will be able to estimate the value of his work in the islands, so great was it. To my knowledge, even to this day, the natives regard him as some great soul who had been specially sent down to them straight from the presence of God.' The pity of it was that his stay was so brief. What with the cruel climate and the desolating calamities, his health was swiftly undermined. To his unspeakable sorrow, and to the grief of all upon the islands, he was compelled, after a few years' ministry, to bid his South Sea savages a heart-breaking farewell. He came back to Australia to die.

IV

The last years of his life were spent at Wentworth Falls, in the Blue Mountains, close to the little cemetery in which we have already seen his tomb. To this day the people of the place speak of his sojourn there in the reverential tones in which they would tell of some hallowed and beautiful tradition. Although so pitifully frail, he was the friend of everybody; his kindnesses were countless; and his medical skill was ever at the disposal of the poor. Moreover, it was among these mountains that he imposed upon himself that lovely sunset ministry of his—his ministry to the swagmen. The swagman cuts a picturesque figure in Australian life and literature. He is the gipsy of the south. Roderic Quinn has described him: 'With no companion, except, perhaps, a dog trotting at his heels, he trudges up and down road and track and route, through drought and flood, fair weather and foul, from year's end to year's end. Attuned to the vast distances and the vast silences in which he moves and has his being, he lives and dreams, indifferent to the clamor of the great, weary, working world which he has left behind him.' Everybody in Australia knows the swagman.

Sitting by the side of the road, watching hundreds of these men go by, Dr. Lamb's thoughts flew back across the years, and he seemed to see that pair of tired pilgrims as, half a century before, they passed this very spot. These men who now tramped their way along the dusty road were just as friendless and just as cheerless as those two wayfarers whose memory was so dear to him. Could he do nothing to make the lives of these wanderers less drab? Sauntering along the road, he came upon the log at the corner of the cemetery, and resolved to make it his headquarters. In those days it lay under the pleasant shade of a fine old tree, which has since been removed to make way for the electric wires. The situation had the advantage of being at the bend of the road. He could see a good distance in both directions, and be prepared worthily to entertain a coming guest. Here, morning by morning, he took up his station, waiting for his swagmen to approach him. In one pocket he carried a few packets of cigarettes, plugs of tobacco and boxes of matches; the other bulged out with its stock of New Testaments. Whenever a swagman came along the road, the doctor asked him to share his log. Offering him a smoke, he soon engaged his visitor in delightful conversation. The doctor would listen sympathetically to the recital of the swagman's experiences; and then, in his turn, he would electrify and enthrall his companion by describing his own adventures on the islands and at sea. Then, very deftly, the doctor would turn the conversation to still loftier themes. He would present his new acquaintance with a copy of the New Testament, and would read to him the Saviour's gracious invitation to *the weary* and *the heavy-laden*. For, if anybody knows what it is to be *weary and heavy-laden,* the swagman does.

For some months, the doctor climbed the hill every morning and walked back every night. Then, his strength slowly ebbing, he engaged a barouche from the village inn to drive him to his log after breakfast; but, with the aid of a stick, he still managed to walk back to his home in the dusk. Later still, however, he had to engage the barouche for both journeys. And then the stern logic of events forced him to face another problem. It was clear that the old log under the gum-tree would soon see him for the last time. How, he asked himself, how could he continue his work when compelled to lie in his bed—or in his grave? He had refused to be daunted by a relentless disease. Disappointed in the islands, he had found work to do in the mountains. Why should he permit a premature death to interrupt the programme of his life? With splendid daring, he hurled defiance at the powers of death. He challenged the finality of the tomb. And the records show that his audacity was magnificently vindicated.

V

The time soon came when he could not leave his bed. It was then that he asked for paper and designed his tombstone—the tombstone with *the text*. He ordained that it was to stand at the corner of the cemetery, close to the log on which he had so often sat. It was to be a noble piece of masonry, capable of enduring for centuries. On the *east* and the *west* and the *south* sides of it, there were to be inscribed his name, the names of his twin boys, and several appropriate passages of Scripture. But on the *north* side—the side facing the road—the side that every passing swagman would see—there were to be inscribed these striking and impressive words,

COME UNTO ME, ALL YE THAT LABOR AND ARE HEAVY-LADEN, AND I WILL GIVE YOU REST. TAKE MY YOKE UPON YOU, FOR MY SHOULDER-GEAR IS EASY AND MY SWAG IS LIGHT.

My shoulder-gear is easy and my swag is light! Robert Lamb died at forty-five, and his last thought was for the dust-stained and foot-sore swagman, who, tired of humping his swag, and tired of asking for work, trudged his cheerless way along the endless roads.

VI

My shoulder-gear is easy and my swag is light. If ever there was a man whose load seemed too heavy for his back, and whose shoulders seemed galled by the straps, it was Robert Lamb. But he ridiculed the bare idea. His work was a revelry to him. He fell in love with his savages and his swagmen; and love makes every burden light. We are all fond of the little ragged girl with whom Dr. Guthrie remonstrated. She was carrying a boy almost as big as herself. 'Oh,' she laughed, 'he's no heavy: he's my brither!' His own heart aflame with the love of Christ, Robert Lamb really loved his wild Hebridean savages and his rough Australian swagmen; and, as a natural consequence, love made his shoulder-gear wonderfully easy and his swag surprisingly light.

'Savages!' he would say, when people condoled with him at having had to labor among such ferocious tribesmen, 'it's too bad to call them savages. They need knowing, that's all!' And he drew a comparison between the men among whom he had labored in his missionary days and the mountains among which he now lived. 'To the eye of a tired traveller,' he said, 'these mountains are clad with nothing but gum-trees, grey, monotonous, sombre. But that is Nature's overall. Live here, and she will fill these vast chasms with heaven's own dyes of amethyst and blue, and lead you by mysterious paths to caves and waterfalls, to nymph-haunted dells and fairy-bowers that fill Australian hearts with pride. So is it with the so-called savages, if only you take the trouble to know them.' To such a spirit, the yoke is always easy, the burden always light.

VII

By means of the tombstone, or, at least, by means of *the text* on the tombstone, Robert Lamb thought to defy the tyranny of the tomb and go on with his work when death had done its worst. Was the strategy successful? Let me close with two stories.

1. Mrs. Lamb now resides in Scotland. A year or two ago she visited Australia, and, one beautiful Sunday morning, paid a pilgrimage to her husband's grave. On the stone she found a tin of water containing some wild flowers, neatly arranged. Tied to the flowers was a leaf from a Roman

Catholic prayer-book. Above the printed prayer was written in pencil, *'A tribute from a passing swagman; may the Lord have mercy on his soul.'* Mrs. Lamb reverently folded the paper and took it with her; it is one of her most cherished possessions: it reminds her that her husband is still carrying on his work.

2. Near to the tomb of Robert Lamb is the grave of a little boy. He was so terribly afflicted, both in mind and body, that his poor parents, although feeling for him that peculiar tenderness which such sufferers invariably elicit, were thankful when at last they could lay his tortured frame to rest in this quiet and charming spot. He spent his last summer at Wentworth Falls. Dr. Lamb's tomb acquired an extraordinary fascination for him. 'He would creep away to the little god's-acre,' his father tells me, 'and, very laboriously—for hand and brain had lost their cunning—would copy out the inscription from the tombstone. We little thought at the time that he was soon to have a small grave of his own in that bush cemetery.'

'Come unto Me!' said the Saviour. And the studious young New Zealander came.

'Take My yoke!' said the Saviour. And the earnest young graduate took it.

And he found the straps so easy and the swag so light that his only fear was lest the delightful load should—in this world or in any other—be lifted from his shoulders.

8

PHILIP MELANCTHON'S TEXT
1497–1560
German Protestant reformer and protégé of Martin Luther.

Romans 8:31

I

IT still stands, the old house at Wittenberg, in which, four centuries ago, Philip Melancthon lived and labored. And there, inscribed in bold letters above his study door, is Philip Melancthon's *text!* Melancthon is the most lovable of all the reformers. He is gentle, winsome, unassuming and scholarly. His friend Camerarius has left us a charming picture of Philip's boyhood. We seem to have actually looked into the innocent face and deep-set eyes of the young chorister as, to the delight of all the worshipers, he lifts up his rich clear voice in the choir of the village church at Breton, in the beautiful Rhine country. In those days his frank simplicity and brooding seriousness won the affection of all who met him; his alert and enquiring mind was the admiration of all his instructors; his sensitive spirit and clinging nature conquered every heart. In later life it was his fate to be overshadowed, and he submitted to the process with the ungrudging cheerfulness of a great and generous spirit. He was hidden from the public view behind the massive personality of Martin Luther; but he was never for a

moment concealed from Luther's view. Luther
knew that Melancthon was all gold, and he never
attempted to disguise his appreciation of his worth.
That was a day never to be forgotten when Melancthon discovered, and showed Luther, that the word
that had always been translated *penance* really
meant *repentance, a change of heart.* The two men
were made for each other. 'I am rough, boisterous
and stormy,' writes Luther. 'I am born to fight
against innumerable monsters and devils. I must
remove stumps and stones, cut away thistles and
thorns, and clear the wild forests. But Master
Philip comes along gently and softly, sowing and
watering with joy, according to the gifts which God
has abundantly bestowed upon him.' Melancthon,
in his turn, revelled in Luther's transcendent immensity. Melancthon was essentially a hero-wor-
shipper, and Luther was his hero. 'If,' he writes,
'there is any one whom I dearly love, and whom I
embrace with my whole heart, it is Martin Luther.'
In his *Life of Melancthon,* Professor J. W. Richard
points out that 'by his fiery eloquence, his genial
humor, and his commanding personality, *Luther*
commended the Reformation to the *people.* By his
moderation, his love of order, and his profound
scholarship, *Melancthon* won for it the support of
the *learned.* Lovely and pleasant in their lives, they
toiled, prayed, and suffered for the same great cause,
and in death they are not divided.' When Luther
died, it was Melancthon who pronounced the historic

oration over his tomb. And when, a few years later, Melancthon followed him, his body was lowered into the same grave. They sleep side by side in the old Castle Church at Wittenberg, the church on whose door Luther nailed his famous theses when he sounded, for the first time, the battle-cry of the Reformation.

II

High up on the front of this old house at Wittenberg you may read the inscription: *Here lived, taught and died Philip Melancthon.* For forty years this was his home. He loved every stick and stone about the place. In the summer time he gathered his students about him in the garden, and was always sorry when the approach of winter drove them indoors. His study was the front room on the second floor. See the inscription! *At this place Melancthon, with his eyes turned towards the north, wrote those works which the world now holds in high esteem.* And this other! *Stop, traveller! Against this wall stood the couch on which the venerable Philip Melancthon piously and peacefully died, April* 19, 1560, *at a quarter-past seven o'clock.* Yes, against this wall stood the couch! It was a little travelling-bed that he always took with him on his journeys. When he felt himself failing, he expressed a strong desire to die in his study, within sight of his books. The room seemed haunted by the faces of the students who had gathered round him there. 'Un-

fold my little travelling-bed,' he said, 'and stand it
against the wall. I need it now, for I am going on
the longest journey of all!' The nineteenth of April
was a delicious spring day. The dying man looked
wistfully towards the open window, and smiled as
there floated into the quiet room the song of the
birds he loved so well. In the afternoon, Paul Eber,
his minister, called and read to him his favorite
passages. Like most of us, Philip Melancthon had
several Scriptures that were particularly dear to
him; but *one* stood out from all the rest.

'Read those words again!' he exclaimed, inter-
rupting the minister's recital of the eighth of
Romans.

'If God be for us, who can be against us?' the
minister repeated.

'Ah, that's it! That's it!' murmured Melancthon,
in a kind of ecstasy. *'If God be for us, who can be
against us?'*

The words had always been an infinite comfort to
him. In his correspondence, in his lectures, and in
his table-talk, you will find them quoted more frequently than any others. In the darkest hours of
his life, when powerful foes had threatened to destroy him, and powerful friends had scowled upon
and forsaken him, he had solaced himself repeatedly
with that reflection: *'If God be for us, who can be
against us?'* When Luther died, and it seemed as
though the sacred cause for which they had con-
tended must collapse, he again drew courage from

the same inspired source: *'If God be for us, who can be against us?'* The words even wove themselves into the shadowy fabric of his dreams, and he frequently awoke repeating them. In the last night of his life he fancied that he saw the noble words written in letters of flame before his eyes: *'If God be for us, who can be against us?'*

And those are the words which, in Latin, you will find inscribed over his study door in the old house at Wittenberg: *Si Deus pro nobis, quis contra nos?* For *that* is Philip Melancthon's text!

III

Philip Melancthon died in 1560. Exactly a hundred years later, in 1660, John Bunyan bends over the manuscript of *Grace Abounding.* 'I was brought into great straits,' he tells us. For a while he was afraid that his health might sink under the strain to which he was exposed; he felt that he was threatened by a premature death; and he was not ready to die. But neither was he ready to live! If he lived, he reflected, he might lose such faith as he had. He had seen many, whose love for Christ was once white-hot, grow cool with the passage of the years. It was whilst he was being tossed on the horns of this dilemma that the text which, a century earlier, had thrilled Melancthon with the exultation of triumph, rushed to his rescue. 'I remember,' he says, 'that, as I was sitting in a neighbor's house, and was very sad, that word came suddenly to me: *What shall we say to these things? If God be for us, who can be against us?* That was a help to me.' Of course it was! It was just the word that he needed.

'What shall I say to *Death?*' asked Philip Melancthon, that day in 1560, when Death came knocking at that study door.

'What shall I say to *Life?*' asked John Bunyan, that day in 1660, when Life threatened gradually to sap away his faith.

'What shall we then say to these things?' replies Paul. *'If God be for us, who can be against us?'* It is the only reply possible; and, when that word has been clearly spoken, nothing else remains to be said.

IV

Exactly a century intervened, as we have seen, between the ministry of the text to Philip Melancthon and the ministry of the text to John Bunyan. By an interesting coincidence, I find another century intervening between two other historic occasions on which the text played a conspicuous and memorable part.

Everybody who has read Macaulay's *History of England* will remember his description of the Battle of the Boyne. 'The first of July dawned; a day which has never since returned without exciting strong emotions of very different kinds in the two populations which divide Ireland. The sun rose bright and cloudless. Soon after four, both armies

were in motion.' But, early as was the hour, William of Orange did not enter upon the engagements
of that fateful day until he had assembled his
troops and read to them the words that he desired
them to carry in their hearts through all the excite-
ments and engagements of the day just dawning.
With the solemnity that becomes men going into
action, they stood with bared heads before him.
'What shall we then say to these things?' he read.
And there was a ring of triumph in his voice as he
continued: *'If God be for us, who can be against
us?'* When Lord Carson visited Ballymena some
time ago he was presented by Mr. John Collins with
a Bible in which that text was specially marked and
that memory vividly recalled.

A hundred years after the Battle of the Boyne,
John Wesley was drawing to the end of his days.
On his death-bed he thought of William Wilberforce and of the gallant but apparently hopeless
struggle by which that dauntless reformer was en-
deavoring to overthrow slavery. Mr. Wesley determined to send him a message of encouragement.
'My dear sir,' he wrote, 'unless the divine power
has raised you up to be, like Athanasius, against the
world, I see not how you can go through with your
glorious enterprise in opposing that execrable vil-
lany which is the scandal of religion, of England,
and of human nature. Unless God has raised you
up for this very thing, you will be worn out by the
opposition of men and devils. But, *if God be for us,*

who can be against us? Are all of them together
stronger than He? Go on in the name of God!'

The music of Melancthon's text was always singing itself over and over in John Wesley's heart,
especially towards the end. It soothed his latest
moments. 'A little after,' so runs the account of
the closing scene, 'a little after, a person coming in,
he strove to speak, but could not. Finding they
could not understand him, he paused a little, and
then, with all his remaining strength, cried out:
"The best of all is, God is with us!" and, soon after,
lifting up his dying arm in token of victory, and
raising his feeble voice with a holy triumph not to
be expressed, he again repeated the heart-reviving
words, "The best of all is, God is with us!"'

God is with us! God is with us! And *if God be
for us, who can be against us?*

'What shall we then say to these things?' asked
Philip Melancthon as, in 1560, he looked into the
face of Death. *'If God be for us, who can be against
us?'*

'What shall we then say to these things?' asked
John Bunyan, as, in 1660, he looked into the face of
Life. *'If God be for us, who can be against us?'*

'What shall we then say to these things?' asked
William of Orange, as he surveyed the hosts drawn
up in battle array against him. *'If God be for us,
who can be against us?'*

'What shall we then say to these things?' asked
John Wesley, as, a century later, he reviewed the

mighty forces that band themselves together to re-
sist any vital reform. *'If God be for us, who can be
against us?'*

And so, over and over and over again, the text
that stands inscribed over that old study door at
Wittenberg has played its part bravely in the making
of world-history.

V

Philip Melancthon's text represents a fascinating
study of the *pros* and *cons* of life—the things that
are *for* us and the things that are *against* us. Paul's
conceptions were always continental. They bewilder
us by their immensity. Analysing the universe, he
finds in it two groups of forces; and, in each group,
a league or confederacy exists. Reviewing the first
group, he sees that all things are working; they are
working in concert; and they are working together
for good. A sacred conspiracy is afoot. The stars
above our heads are in secret alliance with the stones
beneath our feet: the sea is in league with the land;
the night has an understanding with the day. All
things are banded, and banded for good.

But the insurrectionary forces in life are also
leagued, he says. He mentions them one by one;
musters them in terrifying array; and shows how
mighty they are—*or seem.* And then, by a magic
touch, he scornfully reveals their paltriness, their
pettiness, their essential triviality. Formidable as
they at first appear, they dwindle into insignificance

when compared with the powers that make for
righteousness. It is the story of Elisha and his
servant over again. When the young man looked
upon the cordon of the Syrians lying along the valley, he cried, 'My master, my master, what shall we
do?' But when, his eyes having been enlightened
in response to the prophet's prayer, he saw the
mountains full of horses and chariots of fire gathered for his protection, he recognized that the
powers that were *for* him were incomparably might-
ier than the hordes that were assembled *against* him.
The secret lies embedded in the heart of Philip
Melancthon's text. The quieter forces are in league
with the divine. The man who ranges himself on
the side of goodness and of God links his life with
omnipotence and secures for himself the serene confidence of ultimate triumph. The sensational feature of every illumination is the discovery that the
insurrectionary forces in life are so feeble and the
nobler forces so overwhelming. Paul draws up his
fearful array of the powers that threaten to destroy
us. And then he speaks of the forces pledged to
our defence. And among those allied forces is—
GOD! *'What shall we then say to these things?'* he
asks. *'If God be for us, who can be against us?'*
The argument is irresistible.

VI

And what then? The logic of the situation is
unmistakable. During a crisis in the American

Civil War, a timid soul sought an interview with Abraham Lincoln.

'Oh, Mr. President,' he exclaimed, 'I am most anxious that the Lord should be on our side!'

'Well,' replied Mr. Lincoln, 'strangely enough, that gives me no anxiety at all. The thing I worry about is to make sure that *I* am on *the Lord's side!*'

That is the question. The divine position is a fixture; mine is plastic. Who is on the Lord's side? That man has principalities and powers banded for his eternal security. Nothing can harm him in this world or in any other. *God is for him: who can be against him?*

9

JOHN BRIGHT'S TEXT

1811–1889

English orator and statesman.

Matthew 5:3–11

I

THE only geographical discovery that could fittingly be named after John Bright would be a range of sky-piercing and snow-capped mountains. As you contemplate his burly figure—bold, resolute, almost defiant—and as you gaze upon his leonine head, crowned during his later and greater years with hair of snowy whiteness, the comparison is simply forced upon you. Everything about him is massive, majestic, mountainous. In his company—even in the company of his biography—you feel that you are among the beetling crags, the rugged slopes, the scarped peaks, the grand and awful summits. In her *Records of a Quaker Family*, Mrs. Boyce casually observes that the physical appearance of John Bright stood out in strong and striking contrast against that of most of the young Quakers of his time. The prevailing type, she says, was tall, thin, long-faced and regular-featured. But Bright's robust figure, his strength of chest and limb, his honest face and resolute carriage—the head thrown defiantly back; the sensitive mouth set as firmly as if he were facing a howling mob or standing at the bar of a hostile court—reminded you of the stalwart leaders of classical times.

> So sturdy Cromwell pushed broad-shouldered on;
> So burly Luther breasted Babylon!

Moreover, his life is in keeping with his looks. The heroic achievements of his illustrious career— his gallant fight for the food of the people; his fear- less championship of the American slave; his stub- born insistence on the enfranchisement of the cot- tager; his uncompromising stand for civil and re- ligious liberty; his dauntless struggle on behalf of European peace—tower up before the fancy of the student of his life-story like the virgin summits of the Himalayas. His character, as Mr. Gladstone feelingly remarked in the House of Commons, his character is one which we instinctively regard, not merely with admiration, nor even with gratitude, but with reverential contemplation. Mr. Gladstone's phrase reminds me of the awe that has often hushed my soul into silence as, in New Zealand, I have gazed upon the white, white mountains. Bright's form is mountainous; his mind is mountainous. His very speech is mountainous. He stands firm-footed and square-shouldered before his audience, solid and sta- tionary. He never ramps, never raves, never screams, never storms. He seldom moves a foot or waves a hand. Yet he 'awes his listeners by the very calm of his passion.' His views, as Mr. Trevel- yan finely says, are as limpid and resistant as a block

of crystal. In reading his record, we are exploring
the ranges all the time.

II

Yes, we are among the mountains; and the mountains are the home of mystery. The eternal hills
subdue us by their silence. They seem to nurse a
secret. So did John Bright. He impressed men by
his very quietude; his stillness was the eloquent expression of his strength; his great soul seemed to
gather calm and courage from a vision of other
worlds. Mr. Augustine Birrell always felt that the
attitude of Mr. Bright's mind was that of a solitary;
he seemed to be brooding on thoughts too vast for
utterance; he literally walked with God. 'Deep in
his heart,' his biographer tells us, 'there lies always
something unseen, something reserved and solitary.
Although he was a popular hero, and a man so
sociable that he never travelled by train but he drew
into conversation his chance carriage companions;
though he was always happy and tender and talk-
ative when wife or child or friend were near, yet the
presence of an inner life of deep feeling and medi-
tation could be felt as the moving power of all that
he did.'

A secret!
A something unseen!
An inner life of deep feeling!

But the most impressive witness as to all this is
Lord Morley, then plain John Morley. Everybody

knows Lord Morley's attitude towards religion. But
Lord Morley, in his *Voltaire,* tells us that the brilliant Frenchman was more affected by the transparent sincerity and simple piety of the English
Quakers than by all the arguments for Christianity
advanced by the schoolmen. Lord Morley may
have been speaking feelingly, for he himself confessed that 'the most pure and impressive piece of
religion that he ever witnessed was John Bright
reading a chapter of the Bible to his maid-servants
shortly after his wife's death, in his beautiful and
feeling voice, followed by a Quaker silence.' Lord
Morley ranks John Bright with John Hampden,
John Selden, John Pym and the great Puritans,
men who, in Macaulay's classic phrase, 'were not
content to catch occasional glimpses of the Deity
through an obscuring veil, but aspired to gaze full
on His intolerable brightness and commune with
Him face to face.' 'It was this,' says Lord Morley,
'that made John Bright the glory of the House of
Commons.' He sometimes startled men by unex-
pectedly drawing the veil and revealing the imma-
nence of the unseen and eternal. Dr. Dale describes
one of his great orations. It was delivered in the
Birmingham Town Hall. The chairs had been removed so that as many as possible could be crowded
into the building. Five thousand men stood on the
floor, packed so tightly that they could not raise
their hands from their sides to applaud. Mr. Bright
had recently been ill; and he began by reverently

expressing his gratitude to God for his recovery. Dr. Dale says that the hush that fell on the vast and excited assembly as soon as he began to speak deepened into awe. 'We had expected a fierce assault on his political opponents; but the storms of party passion were for a moment stilled; we suddenly found ourselves in the presence of the eternal, and some of us, perhaps, rebuked ourselves in the words of the patriarch, *"Surely the Lord is in this place and I knew it not!"* '

Here, then, is the man—a mountainous man—a man who, like the mountains, lifts his head to the skies and cherishes in solitude a wondrous secret. Now what is that secret? And how and when did he learn it? And what if the secret prove to be a text?

III

John Bright's text was as mountainous as the man himself, as mountainous as everything about him. For John Bright's text was *the Sermon on the Mount*. And the *Sermon on the Mount* was not only delivered on a Mount; it *is* a Mount. It is a lofty eminence standing out boldly against the sky-line of all our little earthly horizons; it is a range of sunlit heights whose terrific grandeur has taunted and challenged and beckoned the pilgrims of the ages. And if, as they essayed the superb adventure, they sometimes scaled the slopes with aching sinews and with bleeding feet, they nevertheless struggled bravely upwards with eager hearts and radiant faces.

The public life of John Bright was, as he himself put it, one long endeavor to inscribe the *Sermon on the Mount* on the pages of the Statute Book. No man of his time could quote Scripture as John Bright could quote it. When it was whispered through the lobbies of the House of Commons that 'Bright was up,' the chamber instantly filled. Lord Morley considers him the stateliest and most finished orator to whom the House of Commons has ever listened. 'I have met men,' he says, 'who have heard Pitt and Fox, and in whose judgment *their* eloquence at its best was inferior to the finest efforts of John Bright.' And, by universal consent, the most impressive passages in those masterpieces of English rhetoric were his appeals to the majesty and authority of Scripture. In his deep voice and with his simple dignity, he would cite some noble phrase from prophet or psalmist or seer; and his hearers would somehow feel that he had lifted the question beyond the range of argument. A gentleman who heard him speak at Bradford in 1877 wrote to a London paper in 1909 to say that he could never forget how Mr. Bright's voice swelled and grew in depth and volume, as it was wont to do when he was deeply moved, as he referred to the *Sermon on the Mount*. Mr. Bright repeated, as only he could have done, the blessings uttered by the divine lips upon the Poor in Spirit, the Mourners, the Meek, the Hungerers after Righteousness, the Merciful, the Pure in Heart and the Peacemakers; and then, having impressively recited these Beatitudes and quoted other appropriate expressions from the *Sermon on the Mount,* he summed up his aim, and that of his associates, by saying, *'We have tried to put Holy Writ into an Act of Parliament!'*

His friendship with Cobden—one of the most potent factors in his career—culminated in an incident in which the *Sermon on the Mount* figures conspicuously. It was Cobden who gave Bright his mission. The story is very familiar: it is one of the most tender idylls in the public life of England. Bright's beautiful young wife, to whom he was devotedly attached, had been suddenly snatched from him. Bright was inconsolable. Let him tell his own story. 'It was in 1841,' he says. 'The sufferings throughout the country were fearful. I was at Leamington, and, on the day when Cobden called upon me—for he happened to be there at the time on a visit to some relatives—I was in the depths of grief, I might almost say despair; for the light and sunshine of my house had been extinguished. All that was left on earth of my young wife, except the memory of a sainted life and a too brief happiness, was lying still and cold in the chamber above us. Mr. Cobden called upon me, and addressed me, as you might suppose, with words of condolence. After a time he looked up and said, "There are thousands of houses in England at this moment where wives,

mothers and children are dying of hunger. Now,"
he said, "when the first paroxysm of your grief is
past, I would advise you to come with me, and we
will never rest till the Corn Law is repealed." I
accepted his invitation. I knew that the description
he had given of the homes of thousands was not an
exaggerated description. I felt in my conscience
that this was a work which somebody must do, and
therefore I accepted his invitation, and from that
time we never ceased to labor hard in fulfilment of
the resolution which we had made.' During the
seven years that followed, the reformers endured
every form of ignominy, ridicule and persecution,
but they struggled on until their cause was triumphant and the whole world was ringing with their
fame.

A few years later, Bright is again overwhelmed
with grief. Cobden himself is dead. John Bright
is in the darkened home. 'This morning,' he says,
'I spent a long time, probably near two hours, in the
library where the body is, with the children. Standing by me, and leaning on the coffin, was his sorrow-
ing daughter, one whose attachment to her father
seems to have been a passion scarcely equalled
amongst daughters. She said, "My father used to
like me very much to read to him the *Sermon on the
Mount;* he said it was so very beautiful." His own
life was to a large extent a sermon based upon that
text, the greatest of all sermons; his life was a life
of perpetual self-sacrifice.' I have sometimes won-

dered whether Cobden's fondness for the *Sermon on the Mount* was the result of his intimacy with Bright. At any rate, the terms in which Mr. Bright records the incident sufficiently reflect the reverent affection that he always cherished for that monumental fragment of sacred literature.

IV

There is an old legend of a boy who gazed so frequently and so steadfastly at the portrait of a face that he admired, that, little by little, his own features came to resemble those in the painting. Something of the kind happened in the case of John Bright. He not only loved the *Sermon on the Mount:* he *became* the *Sermon on the Mount*. 'The *Sermon on the Mount*,' says a well-known commentator, 'stands between the Old Testament and the New; and it gathers to itself all that is best in both.' Strangely enough, John Bright's biographer makes a very similar remark in reference to him. 'In him were blended,' says Mr. Trevelyan, 'the Old Testament and the New, the two indispensable contradictories that man must learn to reconcile within his breast. By careful search, some rudiments of these two opposites can be found in each of us, but in none did they come to such double perfection as in John Bright.' Men who loved the *Sermon on the Mount* delighted in his company; men who would have been rebuked by its perusal were rebuked by his silent presence. The *Life of John Bright* is the finest commentary on the *Sermon on the Mount* that has ever been published. One of these days some commanding literary genius will give us a volume containing the *Sermon on the Mount,* sentence by sentence, and, against each sentence, he will reproduce some speedily illuminative extract from the speeches or biography of John Bright. This is how he will go about it:

Blessed are the Poor in Spirit, says the first clause of the *Sermon on the Mount.* And, against it, our littérateur will give the passage telling of Mr. Bright's ceaseless ministry to the cripple woman among the Welsh hills. Or, if he prefers an extract from one of his hero's election speeches, he will give us this passage delivered at Durham. 'Rich and great people can take care of themselves,' said Mr. Bright, 'but the poor and defenceless—the men with small cottages and large families—the men who must work six full days every week if they are to live in anything like comfort for a week—these men want defenders; they want champions to state their case in Parliament; they want men who will protest against any infringement of their rights.'

Blessed are the Merciful, says the *Sermon on the Mount.* When Sir Henry Hawkins was made a judge—and he became the greatest criminal judge that our courts have ever known—he met John Bright at dinner. Sir Henry told Mr. Bright of his elevation, and expected his congratulations. 'But,' says Sir Henry, 'he simply put his hand on my shoulder, and, in a voice of deep emotion, said, "Be merciful, Hawkins, be merciful!" ' And anybody who cares to look up a certain issue of *Punch,* published in February, 1887, will find a particularly beautiful poem in celebration of the skill with which Sir Henry mingled mercy with justice.

Blessed are the Peacemakers, says the *Sermon on the Mount.* When, in 1855, the nation was swept off its feet by the fever of war, Bright brought upon himself the furious indignation of the whole community by his passionate pleadings for peace. 'The Angel of Death is abroad throughout the land,' he exclaimed in the House of Commons, and, amidst a tense and strained silence, in the course of which he glanced at the vacant seats of members who had fallen, he added, 'you may almost hear the beating of his wings!' 'After the speech,' Bright told a friend, 'I went into Bellamy's to have a chop. Disraeli came and sat down beside me. "Bright," he said, "I would give all that I ever had to have made the speech that you made just now!" '

Blessed are the Pure in Heart, says the *Sermon on the Mount.* John Bright loved all pure and beautiful things. 'He never tired of the sight of mountain and stream,' says Mr. Trevelyan, 'or of the sound of Milton and the Bible passages.' The last photograph ever taken of him represents him with his arm round his little granddaughter; and the last half-conscious caress of his dying hand rested on the head of his little dog 'Fly.'

And so one might go on to the end. For the *Sermon on the Mount* ends with the Parable of the Two Builders, one of whom reared his house on the rock and the other on the sand. If ever there was a man who founded all of his hope for time and for eternity upon the Rock—the Rock of Ages—it was John Bright. And when the storms came—and few men have felt their fury more than he—he was able to face them with a serenity that was unclouded and unruffled.

V

This was his secret. When did he learn it? It is difficult to say. It is always difficult to point to any precise spot among the foothills and to say, *Here* the plain comes to an end and *here* the mountains begin! But those who have caught the spirit of that Quaker home at Rochdale—the home of John Bright's infancy—will understand. When Dr. Oswald Dykes wrote his commentary on the *Sermon on the Mount* he entitled it *The Manifesto of the King*. It is a noble title. From his earliest childhood John Bright was taught the absolute supremacy of Jesus. He crowned Christ Lord of all, and accepted the *Sermon on the Mount* as his Master's royal mandate. Tennyson, his son tells us, had a boundless admiration for the *Sermon on the Mount:* he thought it perfect beyond compare; but he recognized that it involves a man in tremendous obligations.

Man am I grown, a man's work must I do.
Follow the deer? follow the Christ, the King,
Live pure, speak true, right wrong, follow the King—
Else, wherefore born?

That was John Bright's sentiment exactly; in that spirit he lived, in that spirit he labored, and in that spirit he died.

10

JOEY MCQUMPHA'S TEXT

Character in *A Window in Thrums* by J. M. Barrie.

Genesis 16:13

I

JOEY MCQUMPHA was only a little child—a wee Scots laddie—but he had a text; and it was the darling dream of his brief day to be a minister and go into the pulpit and preach on that text. It is Sir J. M. Barrie who, in *A Window in Thrums,* tells Joey's story. At least, Sir J. M. Barrie tells the story of Joey's mother, poor Jess; and it is Jess who tells us all about Joey. The window that gives its name to Sir J. M. Barrie's book is simply the frame in which, to those who pass down the brae, the face of Jess is always set. For Jess is an invalid. With a little help she can just hobble across from the bed to the window; and it is at this window that Jess has sat, day after day, for more than twenty years.

Once, long ago, Jess was taken ill, and the doctor abandoned hope. She called Joey to her bedside and told him that she was going on a long, long journey, and she begged him to be 'a terrible guid laddie' to his father and to Leeby, his sister, after she had gone. Her words, however, failed to produce the effect that she desired. Joey was simply puzzled, bewildered, dumbfounded. His mother, who could scarcely crawl across the room, and who could not even move without her stick, going on a long, long journey! The thing was ridiculous; and, anyhow, he could circumvent any such attempt! He lay awake that night until the house was quiet. And then he rose in the darkness, stole out into the garden, and there, with his little frame shivering and his teeth chattering, he buried his mother's staff among the cabbages! How could she go on a long, long journey without *it?* Happily for Joey, and for his father and sister, Jess did not set out on that long journey after all. It was Joey himself who took it.

'Twenty years have passed,' Sir James tells us, 'since Joey ran down the brae to play. Jess shook her staff fondly at him. A cart rumbled by, the driver nodding on the shaft. It rounded the corner and stopped suddenly, and then a woman screamed. A handful of men carried Joey's dead body to his mother, and *that* was the tragedy of Jess's life.'

And yet there was a sense in which Joey never went out of Jess's life. 'Every other living being forgot him; even to Hendry he became scarcely a name; but there were times when Jess's face quivered and her old arms went out for her dead boy.' On Sundays especially he seemed to creep softly back to her. Jess, of course, could not go to church. But when the others had gone, and the house was still, she and Joey seemed shut up to each other. On those hushed and hallowed mornings, she was

very close to the little boy who died.   She liked
to remember that many a time, after church, he had
run all the way home in order to get to her as quickly
as possible, and had stood beside her chair waving
his hands in a reverent way just like the minister.
Jamie, her other boy, had always prattled about
keeping a shop; but Joey never once wavered in his
resolve to be a minister.   He would be a minister,
he used to say, and his first text would be *Thou
God seest me.*

'We'll get a carriage to ye, mother,' he would tell
her, 'so 'at ye can come and hear me preach on
Thou God seest me.   It doesna do, mother, for the
minister in the pulpit to nod to ony o' the folk; but
I'll gie ye a look an' ye'll ken it's me.   Ye'll be
proud o' me, will ye no, mother, when ye see me
comin' sailin' alang to the pulpit in my gown?   The
other folk will be sittin' in their seats wonderin'
what my text's to be; but you'll ken, mother, an'
you'll turn up to *Thou God seest me* afore I gie out
the chapter.'

'Ye'll wonder at me,' Jess would say, twenty years
afterwards, 'but I've sat here in the lang fore-nichts
dreamin' 'at Joey was a grown man noo, an' 'at I
was puttin' on my bonnet to come to the kirk to hear
him preach on *Thou God seest me.*   I used to be
proud to hear him speakin' o' it.   Aye, but that day
he was coffined, for all the minister prayed, I found
it hard to say, *Thou God seest me.*   It's the text I
like best noo, though, an' when Hendry an' Leeby

is at the kirk I turn't up often, often in the Bible. I read frae the beginnin' o' the chapter, but when I come to *Thou God seest me* I stop. Na, it's no'at there's ony rebellion to the Lord in my heart noo, for I ken He was lookin' doon when the cart gaed ower Joey, an' He wanted to tak my laddie to Himself. But juist when I come to *Thou God seest me,* I let the Book lie in my lap, for aince a body's sure o' that they're sure o' all.'

Towards the end of the book, Sir J. M. Barrie tells us how, at length, poor Jess did actually set out on that long, long journey from which, many years before, Joey had tried so hard to turn her. But this time there was no Joey to hide her stick; and, even if the hiding of the stick could have rendered the journey impossible, Joey would not have hidden it; for, this time, the long, long journey was not taking her from him but bringing her to him. Jess outlived her husband and daughter, after all; but her turn came at last. The minister was with her when she died. She was in her chair at the window, and the minister asked her, as was his custom, if there was any particular chapter which she would like him to read. Since her husband's death she had always asked for the fourteenth of John. It was known in Thrums as Hendry's favorite chapter; he had always sought and found refuge there in days of stress and storm. But this time she asked the minister to read the sixteenth of Genesis. It was ever her own favorite.

'Aye, ye'll laugh,' she would sometimes say, 'but I think that, though Joey never lived to preach in a kirk, he's often preached frae *Thou God seest me* to me. I dinna ken 'at I would ever hae been sae sure o' that if it hadna been for him, an' so I think I see him sailin' doon to the pulpit juist as he said he would do. Naebody sees him but me, but I see him gien me the look he spoke o'.'

She asked the minister to read that chapter at the last. 'When I came to the thirteenth verse,' the minister afterwards said, 'and when I read the words *Thou God seest me,* she covered her face with her two hands and said, "Joey's text! Joey's text! Oh, but I grudged ye sair, Joey!" I shut the book when I came to the end of the chapter and then I saw that she was dead.'

Joey's text! Joey's text! Perhaps Sir J. M. Barrie's text!

Thou God seest me! Thou God seest me!

'When I come to "Thou God seest me",' says Jess, 'I let the Book lie in my lap, for aince a body's sure o' that, they're sure o' all!'

I wonder what she meant! We must try to find out!

II

And, to help us in the elucidation of that problem, I propose to call a pair of witnesses, each of them as unlike the other as could possibly be.

The *first* is a Lord Mayor of London.

The *second* is the Mother Superior of a Spanish Convent!

The Lord Mayor of London to whom I refer is Sir William M'Arthur, K.C.M.G., one of England's merchant princes. The name of Sir William M'Arthur is associated, not only with the commercial activities of the huge metropolis whose chief magistrate he became, and one of whose constituencies he represented in the House of Commons, but with the commercial activities of this great Australian city in which I am writing. As early as 1856 he was the head of one of our principal mercantile houses; and few visitors from the Homeland have been shown more signal honor than was he when, in 1878, he visited these shores. Parliaments, corporations and commercial organizations vied with each other in welcoming him to Australia. He became Lord Mayor of London in 1880; and, to celebrate the event, banquets were held simultaneously on both sides of the world. His biography, written by Mr. Thomas McCullagh, lies open on my desk at this moment. As I review Sir William M'Arthur's crowded and useful life; as I survey the world-wide ramifications of his stupendous commercial enterprises; as I recount the exalted public positions that, one after the other, he adorned; as I note his munificent benefactions, his ample philanthropies and his immense influence; above all, when I contemplate his beautiful home life and his simple piety, I find myself in a fever of curiosity to ascer-

tain the secret of so wealthy and fruitful a career.
By what subtle forces was it inaugurated? Mr.
McCullagh confesses his inability to give any precise account of the dawn of faith in his hero's soul.
'To the close of his life,' Mr. McCullagh says, 'Sir
William could not recollect a time when he did not,
through divine grace, love God and trust in Christ
as his personal Saviour.' And, just before his death,
he told the Rev. C. H. Crookshank that he could
point to no particular instrumentality, or mark any
particular time, as the instrumentality and time of
his conversion. 'From earliest years,' says Mr.
Crookshank, 'he appears, like Timothy, to have
known the Scriptures, and to have been surrounded
by gracious influences through which he grew up
in the fear of the Lord.' So far, except in a vague
and general way, my quest for the secret of his
noble life seems fruitless.

Later on, however, I make an illuminating discovery. Sir William died very suddenly in a railway train, on his way to business, at the age of
seventy-eight. In his desk, after his death, was
found a document which he had drawn up as a
youth of twenty, and which he had jealously preserved all through the years. It begins by expressing
his anxiety lest the business life on which he is just
embarking should so excite and engross his attention as to wean his heart away from God. He then
lays down the rules by which his life shall be gov-
erned. And the document ends with a prayer:

'*O Lord God Almighty,*' he cries, '*do Thou enable me to put these resolutions into practice. Grant me the aid of Thy Holy Spirit! Forgive the past and enable me to live to Thee in future, and in all things to promote Thy honor and glory, through Jesus Christ my Lord. Amen.*' And, conspicuously among the rules that he frames for the guidance of his life, I find this:

'I will endeavor to keep a calm recollection of spirit when engaged in purchasing goods, remembering at all times *Thou God seest me.*'

That significant document is dated Manchester, *November* 9, 1830. Exactly fifty years afterwards to the very day—on *November* 9, 1880—Sir William M'Arthur became Lord Mayor of London!

III

It is a far cry from this brilliant banquet at the Guildhall to the hushed seclusion of Santa Teresa's cloister. But the text—the text on which Joey McQumpha was so eager to preach; the text that so strangely comforted poor Jess in the years that followed Joey's death; the text on which Sir William M'Arthur founded his illustrious career—that same text once came with extraordinary grace and power to the anxious and almost despairing Teresa. Although a nun, she had long since given up praying. The frightful aridity of her heart filled her with dread, and she felt that she dared not present herself before the heavenly throne. But *Thou God seest*

me! She *was* in the presence of the Highest,
whether she deliberately sought that presence or
not! 'It was a great act of grace in God to give me
that vision!' she says. 'I believe that, had the Lord
been pleased to send me that great revelation of
Himself earlier in my life, it would have kept me
back from much sin. I knew not where to hide
myself. I could not flee from that presence. Oh,
that those who commit deeds of darkness could see
what I saw! If they could but see that there is no
place secret from God; but that all that they do
is done before Him and in Him! Oh the madness
of committing sin in the immediate presence of a
Majesty so great! In this also I saw His infinite
mercy in that He suffers such a sinner as I am still
to live!'

So much for our pair of witnesses! The striking
and valuable factor in their testimony lies in the fact
that, like Joey McQumpha and his mother, the Lord
Mayor and the Mother Superior both discover
something wonderfully winsome in the text. If only
Joey could have lived and become a minister! If
only he could have preached the sermon that he so
fervently desired to preach! And if only his mother
and Sir William M'Arthur and Santa Teresa could
have been in the kirk that morning! How delighted
all three of them would have been when the young
minister announced his text!

Thou God seest me! I can see old Jess's eyes
sparkle. 'Aye,' she murmurs to herself in a kind

of ecstasy, 'aince a body's sure o' that, they're sure o' all!'

Thou God seest me! Sir William M'Arthur gives a start as, looking into the preacher's glowing face, the old familiar words fall once more upon his ear. He thinks of that mellow document that he himself drafted as a boy. 'I will endeavor to keep a calm recollection of spirit when engaged in purchasing goods, remembering at all times *Thou God seest me!*'

Thou God seest me! A tear glistens on Santa Teresa's cheek as she recalls the vision that helped her back to a life of communion with her Lord!

Thou God seest me! Jess finds in Joey's text an unspeakable comfort. The Lord Mayor finds in Joey's text a life-long inspiration. Santa Teresa finds in Joey's text an infinite mercy. 'In this I saw his infinite mercy in that He suffers me still to live.'

Unspeakable Comfort! Life-long Inspiration! Infinite Mercy! Is it any wonder that Joey McQumpha longed to be a minister and to preach on that great text?

IV

'I used to hate that text!' Bishop Bonner would say, as he pointed to the words that were so dear to Joey and Jess. 'When I was a child and was naughty, my nurse made me repeat it again and again,' the Bishop said, 'and it terrified me!' But, later on, his eyes were opened. He saw in the text all that Joey and Jess and Sir William M'Arthur and Santa Teresa saw in it, and he became as fond of it as they were. The point is, not that I am watched, but that I am watched by One whose name is Love and whose heart is full of compassion. There are some lines by Dr. J. R. Miller which, in the course of his sermon, Joey would not, perhaps, have quoted; but I know that he would have liked to quote them:

> But naebody ever will ken, lassie,
> O naebody ever will ken,
> How much we hide that we canna 'bide
> Should be seen by the eyes o' men, lassie,
> Should be seen by the eyes o' men.
>
> There's One sees thro' an' thro', lassie,
> There's One sees thro' an' thro':
> And better than a', whatever befa',
> He's gentle, an' kind, an' true, lassie,
> He's gentle an' kind an' true.

That's it! *Thou God seest me;* and Thou art gentle an' kind an' true!

Mr. Frederick Mann expresses the same thought:

Thou seest me, O God, and plain beneath Thy sight appear
The tale of years that vanish, and all secrets deep as night;
Thine eyes are searching through me, yet I will not
    shrink nor fear:
Thy heart is full of tenderness, Thine arm of help is near,
    And Thou, O God, art Love as well as Light!

Thou seest me. Each word and inmost thought alike is
    known,
My comings and my goings, though Thyself I cannot see;
Though blindness well might smite me from the light
    before Thy Throne,
My soul bows down to bless Thee for Thou callest me
    Thine own,
      And seeing, yet Thou lovest even me!

The Rev. Joseph McQumpha would have pointed
out, in that sermon that he did not live to preach,
that the eyes that search me through and through
are the eyes that, turning and looking upon Peter,
broke his heart. And, beyond the shadow of a
doubt, there would have been many broken hearts
and contrite spirits in the Rev. Joseph McQumpha's
church that morning.

11

JOHN G. PATON'S TEXT

1824–1907

Pioneer Scottish missionary to the New Hebrides.

Matthew 28:20

I

I CAN see him now, as, stately and patriarchal, he walked up the desk-room of the old college to address us. As that impressive and striking figure appeared at the door, every student instinctively sprang to his feet and remained standing till the Grand Old Man was seated. I thought that I had never seen a face more beautiful, a figure more picturesque. A visitant from another world could scarcely have proved more arresting or awe-inspiring. When it was announced that Dr. J. G. Paton, the veteran missionary to the New Hebrides, was coming to address the college, I expected to *hear* something thrilling and affecting; but, somehow, it did not occur to me that my *eyes* would be captivated as well. But, when the hero of my dreams appeared, a picture which I shall carry with me to my dying day was added to the gallery which my memory treasures. This was in London many years ago. I little thought that afternoon that the apostolic form before me would one day sleep in an Australian grave, and that my own home would stand within half an hour's journey of his lovely resting-place.

In preparation for the task to which I now address myself, I paid a pilgrimage to the Boroondara Cemetery this afternoon, and read Dr. J. G. Paton's text bravely inscribed upon his tomb. It is not the kind of text that is usually engraved upon such monuments, but it is in every way appropriate to *him*. 'In his private conversation,' writes his son, the Rev. F. H. L. Paton, M.A., B.D., 'in his private conversation and in his public addresses, my father was constantly quoting the words, *Lo, I am with you alway,* as the inspiration of his quietness and confidence in time of danger, and of his hope in the face of human impossibilities. So much was this realized by his family that we decided to inscribe that text upon his tomb in the Boroondara Cemetery. It seemed to all of us to sum up the essential element in his faith, and the supreme source of his courage and endurance.'

'Lo, I am with you alway!'
The secret of a quiet heart!
The secret of a gallant spirit!
The secret of a sunny faith!
The text so often on the tongue! The text upon the tomb!
'Lo, I am with you alway, even unto the end!'

II

The text is the tincture of miracle. Edna Lyall once wrote a novel—*We Two*—to show the wondrous magic that slumbers in those sacred syllables.

We Two is the story of Erica Raeburn. Erica is the daughter of Luke Raeburn, the sceptic; and she has been taught from infancy to despise all holy things. But as life, with its stress and struggle, goes on, she finds that she cannot satisfy her soul with denials and negations. 'At last,' Edna Lyall says, 'Erica's hopelessness, her sheer desperation, drove her to cry to the Possibly Existent.' She stood at the open window of her little room, looking out into the summer night. Before she knew what had happened, she was praying!

'O God,' she cried, 'I have no reason to think that Thou art, except that there is such fearful need of Thee. I can see no single proof in all the world that Thou art here. But *if* Thou art, O Father, *if* Thou art, help me to know Thee! Show me what is true!'

A few days later the answer came. Erica was at the British Museum, making some extracts, in the ordinary course of her business, from the *Life of Livingstone*. All at once she came upon the extract from Livingstone's *Journal,* in which he speaks of his absolute reliance upon the text, *Lo, I am with you alway.* 'It is the word,' says Livingstone, 'it is the word of a gentleman of the strictest and most sacred honor, and there's an end of it!' The words profoundly affected Erica. *Lo, I am with you alway!* They represented, not a Moral Principle, nor a Logical Proposition, but a Living Presence!

'Exactly how it came to her, Erica never knew, nor could she put in words the story of the next few minutes. When *God's great sunrise* finds us out, we have need of something higher than human speech; there *are* no words for it. All in a moment, the Christ Who had been to her merely a noble character of ancient history became to her the most real and vital of all living realities. It was like coming into a new world; even dingy Bloomsbury seemed beautiful. Her face was so bright, so like the face of a happy child, that more than one passer-by was startled by it, lifted for a moment from sordid cares into a purer atmosphere.'

All this is in the early part of the book; but even in the last chapter Erica is still rejoicing in her text, and in the deathless treasure which it had so suddenly unfolded to her. *God's great sunrise* had come to stay.

III

God's great sunrise broke upon J. G. Paton amidst the sanctities and simplicities of his Scottish home. He was only a boy when he learned the sublime secret to which the text gives expression, and it was his father who revealed it to him. In a passage that has taken its place among our spiritual classics, he has described the little Dumfriesshire cottage, with its 'but' and its 'ben,' and the tiny apartment in which he used to hear his father at prayer. And whenever the good man issued from that cottage sanctuary, there was a light in his face which, Dr. Paton says, the outside world could never understand; 'but we children knew that it was *a reflection of the Divine Presence in which his life was lived.*'

And, continuing this touching story, Dr. Paton describes the impression that his father's prayers in that little room made upon his boyish mind. 'Never,' he says, 'in temple or cathedral, on mountain or in glen, can I hope to feel that the Lord God is more near, more visibly walking and talking with men, than under that humble cottage roof of thatch and oaken wattles. Though everything else in religion were by some unthinkable catastrophe to be swept out of memory, my soul would wander back to those early scenes, and would shut itself up once again in that sanctuary closet, and, hearing still the echoes of those cries to God, would hurl back all doubt with the victorious appeal: *He walked with God; why may not I?*'

Why, indeed? J. G. Paton resolved that his father's religion should be *his* religion; his father's God *his* God. He pinned his faith to the sublime assurance on which his father rested with such serenity. During all his adventurous years in the South Seas, he relied implicitly upon it, and, as a result, he says that he felt immortal till his work was done. 'Trials and hairbreadth escapes only strengthened my faith and nerved me for more to follow; and they trod swiftly enough upon each other's heels. Without that abiding consciousness of the presence and power of my Lord and Saviour, nothing in the world could have preserved me from losing my reason and perishing miserably. His words *Lo, I am with you alway, even unto the end* became to me so real that it would not have startled me to behold Him, as Stephen did, gazing down upon the scene. It is the sober truth that I had my nearest and most intimate glimpses of the presence of my Lord in those dread moments when musket, club or spear was being levelled at my life.'

Thus, then, J. G. Paton, as a boy in his Scottish home, learned the unutterable value of the text. *Lo, I am with you alway.* Thus, too, twenty years later, he went out to his life-work, singing in his soul those golden words.

IV

He very quickly tested their efficacy and power. It was on the fifth of November, 1858, that the young Scotsman and his wife first landed on Tanna. It was purely a cannibal island in those days, and the white man found his faith in his text severely tried. 'My first impressions,' he tells us, 'drove me to the verge of utter dismay. On beholding the natives in their paint and nakedness and misery, my heart was as full of horror as of pity. Had I given up my much-beloved work, and my dear people in Glasgow, with so many delightful associations, to consecrate my life to these degraded creatures? Was it possible to teach them right and wrong, to Christianize, or even to civilize them?' But this, he goes on to say, was only a passing feeling. He soon reminded himself that he and his wife were not undertaking the work at their own charges. They were not alone. The transformation of the natives seemed impossible; but his son has already told us that the text often braced him to face the apparently impossible. It did then.

If ever a man seemed lonely, J. G. Paton seemed lonely when, three months later, he had to dig with his own hands a grave for his young wife and his baby boy. In spite of all pleas and remonstrances, Mrs. Paton had insisted on accompanying him, and now, the only white man on the island, he was compelled to lay her to rest on this savage spot. 'Let those,' he says, 'who have ever passed through similar darkness—darkness as of midnight—feel for me; as for all others, it would be more than vain to try to paint my sorrows. I was stunned: my reason seemed almost to give way: I built a wall of coral round the grave, and covered the top with beautiful white coral, broken small as gravel; and that spot became my sacred and much-frequented shrine during all the years that, amidst difficulties, dangers and deaths, I labored for the salvation of these savage islanders. Whenever Tanna turns to the Lord and is won for Christ, men will find the memory of that spot still green. It was there that I claimed for God the land in which I had buried my dead with faith and hope.'

With faith and hope! What faith? What hope? It was the faith and the hope of his text! *Lo, I am with you alway!* 'I was never altogether forsaken,' he says, in his story of that dreadful time. 'The ever-merciful Lord sustained me to lay the precious dust of my loved ones in the same quiet grave. But for Jesus, and the fellowship He vouchsafed me there, I must have gone mad and died beside that lonely grave!' A few weeks afterwards, George Augustus Selwyn, the pioneer Bishop of New Zealand, and James Coleridge Patteson, the martyr Bishop of Melanesia, chanced to call at the island. They had met Mrs. Paton—then the picture of perfect health—a few months previously, and were shocked beyond measure to learn the story of the missionary's sorrow. 'Standing with me beside the grave of mother and child,' says Dr. Paton, 'I weeping aloud on his right hand, and Patteson sobbing silently on his left, the good Bishop Selwyn poured out his heart to God amidst sobs and tears, during which he laid his hands on my head and invoked heaven's richest consolations and blessings on me and my trying labors. The virtue of that kind of episcopal consecration I did, and do, most warmly appreciate.' To the end of his days, Dr. Selwyn used to speak of Dr. Paton as one of the bravest and one of the saintliest men he had ever met.

It was thus, at the very outset of his illustrious career, that Dr. Paton discovered the divine dependability of his text.

'Lo, I am with you alway!'

'I was never altogether forsaken!'

'The ever-merciful Lord sustained me!'
'But for Jesus, I must have gone mad and died!'
'Lo, I am with you alway, even unto the end!'

In his extremity, J. G. Paton threw himself upon
the promise; and the promise held.

V

Through the eventful years that followed, the text
was his constant companion. He faces death in a
hundred forms, but the episode invariably closes with
some such record as this:

> During the crisis, I felt generally calm and firm of soul,
> standing erect and with my whole weight on the promise,
> *Lo, I am with you alway.* Precious promise! How often
> I adore Jesus for it and rejoice in it! Blessed be His
> name!

or this:

> I have always felt that His promise, *Lo, I am with you
> alway,* is a reality, and that He is with His servants to
> support and bless them even unto the end of the world.

From many such instances, I cull one as typical of
the rest. In 1862, the whole island was convulsed
by tribal warfare. In their frenzy the natives threatened to destroy both the mission station and the
missionary. Nowar, a friendly chief, urged Dr.
Paton to fly into the bush and hide in a large chestnut tree there. 'Climb up into it,' he said, 'and remain till the moon rises.' He did so, and, concealed

in that leafy shelter, saw the blacks beating the bushes around in their eager search for himself.

'The hours that I spent in that chestnut tree,' writes Dr. Paton, 'still live before me. I heard the frequent discharge of muskets and the hideous yells of the savages. Yet never, in all my sorrows, did my Lord draw nearer to me. I was alone yet not alone. I would cheerfully spend many nights alone in such a tree to feel again my Saviour's spiritual presence as I felt it that night.'

About the hour of midnight a messenger came to advise him to go down to the beach. 'Pleading for my Lord's continued presence, I could but obey. My life now hung on a very slender thread. But my comfort and joy sprang from the words *Lo, I am with you alway.* Pleading this promise, I followed my guide.'

The crisis passed. 'I confess,' Dr. Paton says, 'that I often felt my brain reeling, my sight coming and going, and my knees smiting together when thus brought face to face with a violent death. Still, I was never left without hearing that promise coming up through the darkness and the anguish in all its consoling and supporting power: *Lo, I am with you alway.*'

Some years later, Dr. Paton married again, and settled at Aniwa. But, on a notable occasion, he revisited Tanna. Old Nowar was delighted and begged them to remain.

'We have plenty of food,' he assured Mrs. Paton.

'While I have a yam or a banana, you shall not want.' Mrs. Paton said that she was sure of it.

'We are many!' he cried, pointing to his warriors; 'we are strong; we can always protect you!'

'I am not afraid,' she smilingly replied.

'Then,' says Dr. Paton, 'he led us to that chestnut-tree in the branches of which I had sheltered during that lonely and memorable night when all hope of earthly deliverance had perished, and said to Mrs. Paton, with a manifest touch of genuine emotion, "The God who protected Missi in the tree will always protect you!"'

The Form in the Furnace—the Form that was like unto the Son of God—was seen by Nebuchadnezzar as well as by the Three Hebrew Children. And the Presence of Him who had said *Lo, I am with you alway* was recognized by the barbarians of Tanna, as well as by Dr. Paton himself. Their sharp eyes soon detected that the white man was never left to his own resources.

VI

Dr. Paton lived to be eighty-three, and his promise never failed him. Even when he was weakest, Mr. Langridge says, his heart never doubted for a moment, and, whenever any one came to see him, he rejoiced to tell them how unclouded was the peace within, and how intensely real and sustaining he found the promises of God's Word. He used often to say, 'With me there is not a shadow or a cloud:

all is perfect peace and joy in believing.' A moment after his last breath had been drawn, the lines of pain were smoothed from his fine face, as by an invisible hand. He had actually gazed upon the Saviour, whose vivid presence had been the radiant reality of his life. *God's great sunrise* had broken upon him with even richer splendor; and, as the clouds reflect the afterglow of sunset, so his pale face reflected the afterglow of that beatific vision. He was laid to rest next day in the grave that I visited this afternoon; and now every pilgrim to his sepulchre sees his text boldly inscribed upon his tomb.

12

SANTA TERESA'S TEXT

1515–1582

Spanish Carmelite reformer, mystic, and writer.

John 4:15

I

THE man who has once fallen under the spell of Santa Teresa will carry her image in his heart forever after. Especially will he think of her when he walks beside the sea, strolls along the river bank, or traces the tortuous windings of some upland stream. For, with Teresa, the love of water was a deathless passion. In her romantic pilgrimages along the highways and by-ways of Spain, she would listen entranced if she heard the babble of a brook, the tumbling of a mountain torrent or the deep murmur of a distant waterfall. She thought that earth held nothing more beautiful than the rainbow athwart the spray of a cascade. And whenever, on reaching the crest of a hill, she caught a glimpse of some glassy lake or noble river flashing in the sunlight, she would clap her hands in a frenzy of delight. She loved to bathe her feet in the purling waters; and when, just beside the road, a crystal spring gushed from its nest of ferns and mosses, she gathered her nuns around her, laved her hands in the delicious fountain, and seemed to draw some spiritual refreshment from the sight and sound of the sparkling rill. To the very last, this ruling passion of her life was strong within her. 'Withered and old, and fast nearing the goal of her desires, the windings of the river which she skirted on one of her last journeys on earth—the journey from Plasencia to Soria—roused her enthusiastic admiration.' So says Mrs. Cunninghame Graham, in her *Life and Times of Santa Teresa;* and, later on, she has another striking paragraph. For, on the road to Burgos, Teresa and her nuns are baulked by a river in full flood.

'Now then, my daughters,' cries the intrepid old woman—she is sixty-seven and paralytic at that— 'I will cross first: if I am drowned, you must on no account attempt it!'

So saying, with one of her merry smiles, she plunges boldly into the cauldron of swirling waters and safely reaches the opposite bank. Water is her element: it has no terror for her: she loved it as a little child, and her affection for it remains constant to the last.

With Santa Teresa it was water, water everywhere and water all the time. It was the hearing of a story of the mystic waters that first inclined her heart towards the Saviour. Her teaching is illustrated throughout by the symbolism of the stream. She seems to think in the terms of the pool and the cataract, the well and the shower, the laughing rivulet and the unfathomable ocean depths.

II

It was a great day in the life of Teresa when it first occurred to her that Jesus was as fond of the waters as she was. It was a picture that brought this home to her; and, as long as she lived, she thought of the picture with peculiar fondness and gratitude. It hung in her own room in the home of her girlhood. It represented Jesus resting on the well, talking to the woman of Samaria. 'Oh, how often,' she says in her autobiography, 'how often do I meditate on the living water of which our Lord spoke to the woman of Samaria! That story has a great attraction for me; and, indeed, so it had when I was a little child, though I did not understand it then as I do now. I had in my room a picture representing Jesus at the well. Underneath it, was the inscription: *Lord, give me this water!* I used to kneel down before the picture and pray much to our Lord that I, too, might drink of the wonderful water of which He was speaking.'

It was many years before that girlish prayer was answered; indeed, it was many years before Teresa was ready for the answer. The living water only comes to the thirsty soul; and, as yet, the soul of Teresa knew no such deep and passionate desire. The thought of water fascinated her; the incident depicted in the picture seemed to her very affecting; the Saviour's condescension struck her as exquisitely beautiful; and she felt, in some vague way, that she, too, would like to receive water at His hands; but that was all. Teresa was bubbling over with life and merriment. She was essentially a child of her period; and her period was the gayest and most romantic in Spain's romantic history. She was extraordinarily beautiful—'tall; well-shaped; with a fine complexion; round, brilliant, black eyes; black hair, crisp and curly; good teeth and firmly chiselled lips and nose'—and she quickly learned to display her charms to the best advantage. The frivolity of her girlhood afterwards troubled her. 'I paid a great deal of attention to dress,' she tells us, 'and was anxious that everybody should think me pretty.' She made it her business to keep her small dainty hands most scrupulously white, and she spent a vast amount of time before her mirror in arranging her luxurious black tresses. 'I was fond of perfumes,' she says, 'and of all the vanities within my reach— and they were many—but I had no evil intention in using them.' Of course not. It is with a light and girlish heart that Teresa revels in the flowers and fields and forests about her father's home; it is with a light and girlish heart that she lingers on the image of her graceful form and pretty face as she admires them in the mirror; it is with a light and girlish heart that, at the age of seven, she takes her brother's hand and sets off along the dusty road to Salamanca that they may win for themselves, among the Moors, the glorious crown of martyrdom; and it is with a light and girlish heart that she kneels be-

fore the picture and repeats, over and over and over
again, the prayer inscribed beneath it: *Lord, give me
this water! Lord, give me this water!* 'I did not
understand it then,' she writes, half a century later.
It was not with a light and girlish heart that the
woman in the picture begged for the living water;
it was not with a light and girlish heart that Teresa
herself eventually sought that satisfying stream.

III

Not that Teresa had to surrender her natural
gaiety in order to secure the Saviour's grace. By
no means. Without that gaiety Teresa would not
have been Teresa. She loved water because water
is the natural emblem of vivacity. It ripples and
splashes and foams and thunders: it is full of animation and life. Teresa herself was vivacious to the
end of the chapter. The cloisters of Avila resounded
with her peals of merry laughter. She laughed for
the sheer joy of it when things went well; and mis-
fortunes only appealed to her sense of the ludicrous.
One bitter winter's night, when the poor nuns at
Toledo could not find enough bedclothes to keep
their teeth from chattering, Teresa lit her taper,
went the round of the establishment, poked fun at
the capes, coats, cloths and improvised quilts under
which the girls were shivering, and soon had the
whole place rocking with merriment. When Fray
Juan painted her portrait and brought it to her—
the portrait that still stands as the frontispiece of

her writing and biographies—she broke into immoderate laughter. How could she who had always been so proud of her own loveliness recognize herself in the blear-eyed and hard featured old woman whose grim and heavy visage stared sternly at her from the canvas? Believing, as she said, that God likes to walk among the pots and pipkins, she became a most accomplished cook; but, when a meal was spoiled through some poor sister's blunder in the kitchen, she turned it into a jest at table, and the incident passed in a ripple of silvery mirth. During the fifteen years of her pilgrimages along the great Andalusian highroads, she kept her companions in so blithe a mood that they found it easy to forget their weariness. She cultivated a sharp eye for the whimsical side of every object that they passed; she enlivened every step of the way with clever puns and haunting couplets; for Teresa was a born wit. The most eminent critics agree that the humor of Cervantes is neither more delicious nor more dainty than that of Teresa. She discountenanced all murmurs and complaints, and was never once heard to say an unkind word of anybody. She dearly loved a game: one of her most telling illustrations is drawn from her experiences at chess. Into her convents she introduced musical instruments —the pipe, the flute, the drum, the cymbals, and the tambourine—and trained her nuns to join her in glees and lively melodies; she liked the place to resound with evidence of their mutual happiness.

She could never pass a little child on the road without running to kiss it; she shouted for joy when she caught sight of a brightly-colored butterfly; she liked her nuns to look pretty, and she had nicknames and pet-names for them all.   She did all that she possibly could to keep them blithe.   'No words,' says one of her biographers, 'can give any idea of the glad cheerfulness, the holy joy, the serene composure which reigned in that little world, as it still reigns to-day in many of Teresa's convents. Melancholy in a cloister!   God forbid!   Teresa dreaded the melancholy as the plague; a person infected with it was to be refused admittance to her convents: Teresa liked nuns of clear and serene understandings and unclouded brows.   It never once occurred to Teresa that she was called upon to make a choice between her laughter on the one hand and everlasting life on the other.   'It would be dreadful,' she writes, 'if we could not seek the Saviour until we were dead to this world.   Neither the Magdalen, nor the woman of Samaria, nor she of Canaan, were dead to it when they found Him.'

The woman of Samaria! Teresa's thoughts never wander far from the picture that hung in the old bedroom at home.   No; the woman of Samaria had not lost her love of life.   Was it not *living* water for which she asked?   Wherein, then, lay the difference between the prayer of the little Spanish girl in front of the picture and the prayer of the Samaritan woman in the picture?   Wherein lay the difference between the oft-repeated prayer offered by Teresa as a child—*'Give me this water! give me this water!'*— and the same prayer offered years afterwards by the very self-same lips?

IV

The angel who records earth's requests and heaven's responses would probably tell us that Teresa's later prayer was itself the answer to Teresa's earlier cry. When, as a little girl, Teresa kneeled before the picture, she was not thirsty. She was animated, partly by a child's propensity to imitate its senior, and, partly, by the irresistible fascination that water—a well of water—living water— always had for her. Heaven does not moisten the lips that are not thirsty; but the girlish cry is registered; and, when the thirst comes, the living water is immediately ministered.

The time came when poor Teresa was not only thirsty, but terribly and tragically thirsty. In attempting to describe her sensations, the only symbolism of which she can think is the symbolism of the parched and burning desert. 'O my aridity,' she cries, 'my great and intolerable aridity!' She is a nun, it is true, but she will not be a hypocrite. She abandons prayer as hopeless. How can she pray with her lips when there is no glad and grateful worship welling up from her soul? 'O my God,' she cries, 'I am amazed at the hardness of my wicked heart!' Yet, just as the silence of the desert is

itself one great cry for water, so the silence of
Teresa's soul is but a magnified, intensified echo of
her girlish cry. 'Water! Water! Living water!
Lord, give me this water! give me this water!' And
that passionate cry was heard.

During the years that followed, she wrote a
treatise on the spiritual life—a treatise that still
stands among our choicest religious classics. But,
from the first page to the last, the imagery is colored
by the unforgettable experience of that dreadful
period. She likens the soul to a garden in which
grains and vegetables, beautiful flowers and sweet-
smelling herbs, should flourish. But it is parched
and dry. How is the owner to make it fresh and
fruitful? There are *four* ways, she says. And she
pictures him laboriously drawing water from a well,
becoming exhausted long before the whole garden
has been moistened; again, she pictures him toiling
at a water-wheel with scarcely more success; and, a
third time, she pictures him carrying water to his
garden from a neighboring stream. Then, having,
with a skillful hand, drawn the spiritual analogies in
each case, she proceeds to the *fourth* source of refreshment. The rain; the water that falls from
heaven; the life that comes to the garden from
above! But for it, the well will soon be empty; the
water-wheel will revolve in vain; and the bed of the
stream will be dry. Everything depends upon the
water that must be divinely given. And, with the
old picture in mind, she tells the story of One who

sat by Jacob's well, One to whom the Woman of Samaria—and she herself—had cried: *Lord, give me this water! give me this water!*

V

But, in Teresa's mind, there was a yet deeper resemblance between the woman at the well and herself. The outstanding factor in the New Testament story—the thing that the Samaritan woman herself could never forget—was that Jesus revealed to her her sin—*and forgave it*. In exactly the same way, the outstanding factor in the life of Teresa—the thing that *she* could never forget—was that Jesus had revealed to her *her* sin and forgiven it.

Others called her *'Saint Teresa,'* she signs herself *'Teresa the Sinner.'* As her nuns knelt around her deathbed, she magnified the grace that had dealt so wonderfully with her. 'My children,' she exclaimed, 'I have been the greatest sinner in the world!' And she meant it. She had not sinned as the Woman of Samaria had sinned; Teresa was the soul of purity; her love of water was the expression of her passion for all things clean and cleansing. But, for all that, she was conscious that her soul was soiled. To others, she may have seemed a paragon of virtue; but, as Francis de Sales observes, 'the defects that are scarcely perceptible to the ordinary run of mortals, appear to those who are striving after perfection, as the most grave and heinous transgressions.' 'My wickedness,' cries Teresa, 'ap-

pears to me so enormous that I look upon my sins
as the cause of all the heresy and misery that have
come upon the world.' She had a vision of hell and
she saw her own place in it. The vision was, she
says, one of the greatest mercies that God ever bestowed upon her, for whenever afterwards trials
and sufferings came upon her, she contrasted their
painfulness with the unutterable horror of her
vision. And, even as she gazed upon her place in
that abode of torment, she could not help feeling
that it was pleasant as compared with the still more
dreadful doom that her iniquities deserved. Her
sins were her sorrow day and night. The remem-
brance of them was grievous unto her, the burden
of them was intolerable.

She lost her burden where the Woman of Samaria
lost hers—in the presence of the Saviour. There
came to her, after twenty years of convent life, an
overwhelming vision of the pathos and power of the
Cross. Under such circumstances, as Froude remarks, Protestants and Catholics experience an iden-
tical emotion. 'Each poor sinner recognizes, as by a
flash of lightning, that these tortures were endured
for *him* or *her*—that *he* or *she* was actually present
in the Saviour's mind when He was suffering on
the cross. The thought, when it comes, is over-
powering. Teresa was dissolved in tears. She sur-
rendered herself wholly and forever to the Being
whose form was fastened on her soul. Her spiritual
life had begun.' So Froude tells the story of her

conversion: her own narrative is much more affecting, but it is lengthy. She has seen, so she tells her confessor, the Christ, the living Christ: the sweetness, light and peace that poured themselves into her soul are indescribable; henceforth she can only sing for very gladness: she sings as they alone only can sing to whom much has been forgiven. Teresa has an immense correspondence; but from that time she seals all her communications with a seal that contains five matchless letters—the letters JESUS.

VI

The Woman of Samaria left the well and went back to the world to make history. The whole city was changed as a result of her conversion. So was it with Teresa. She dedicated her transfigured life to the purification and reformation of the religious establishments of Spain; and her work was so wonderful that, when she died, she was made the patron saint of her grateful country. When the time of her departure came, her death was as lovely as her life. She gathered about her the nuns who were as dear to her as daughters. She repeated with them the greatest of our penitential psalms, just such a psalm, as, in dying, the Woman of Samaria might have recited: *'Create in me a clean heart, O God. The sacrifices of God are a broken spirit, a broken and a contrite heart Thou wilt not despise.'* She clung to the words, uttering them again and again

Then 'O my Lord,' she exclaimed, 'the hour that I have so much longed for has come at last: the time has surely come that we shall see one another!' And, with a gentle sigh, she set out—to use her own words—not to a strange country, but to her native land, since it was the land in which *He* dwelt whom she so loved and who so loved her.

13

SYDNEY DOBELL'S TEXT

1824–1874
English poet and critic.

Luke 23:42

I

Is there a preacher living who has not, at some time
or other, felt unutterably thankful that the New
Testament contains the story of the Dying Thief?
Sooner or later there comes to every minister the
experience that, in George Macdonald's *Malcolm,*
came to Mr. Graham, the schoolmaster. The Marquis of Lossie is dying, and, in dying, is desperately
anxious about the salvation of his soul. It seems
to him that the situation is hopeless; it is too late!
'There's no time!' he almost shrieks, 'no time! no
time! *no time!*' And Mr. Graham replies by recit-
ing to his lordship the story of the thief upon the
cross—'that most blessed thief who stole the kingdom of heaven.'

'It makes my heart swell to think of it, my lord,'
says Mr. Graham. 'It is not too late! The Saviour
demands nothing of you which you are not able to
perform! With your last breath you can cry to
Him, and He will hear you, as He heard the thief
who was dying on the cross beside Him. *"Lord,
remember me,"* he cried, *"when Thou comest into
Thy kingdom."* And the Saviour answered, *"To-*

day shalt thou be with Me in Paradise." It makes
my heart swell to think of it! No cross-question-
ing of the poor fellow! No preaching to him! He
just took him with Him where He was going to
make a man of him!'

'To-day,' the Saviour said, '*thou shalt be with Me
in Paradise!*'

' "*To-day!*" exclaims a great French preacher,
'what *promptitude!* "*With Me!*" what *company!*
"*In Paradise!*" what *bliss!*'

'It makes my heart swell to think of it!' says the
schoolmaster; and he is by no means alone. This
tragic but tender story has made its poignant appeal
to men and women of every condition and of every
age. To two classes of people—two classes that
stand in striking contrast the one with the other—
the story has particularly appealed. It has appealed,
on the one hand, to those who, like the Marquis of
Lossie, find themselves faced in their last hour by
a most desperate extremity; and, on the other, it
has appealed to those whose very immunity from
such deplorable conditions has tended to foster a reliance upon their own innocence and goodness. If
ever a mortal was entitled to enter Paradise by
some door other than that by which the Dying Thief
was admitted, it was the Countess of Huntingdon.
The Countess spent all her years, all her strength
and all her fortune in doing good. Yet, when it
came to preparing her soul for the immediate
presence of her Saviour, she found infinite comfort

in the story that made Mr. Graham's heart swell
with thankfulness. 'I have,' the Countess exclaimed,
on the last day of her life, 'I have no hope but
that which inspired the Dying Thief at the side of
my Lord. I must be saved in the same way, as
freely and as fully, or not at all.'

And so the whole story is a study in black and
white, a study in light and shade, a study in sharp
and vivid contrasts. There is the contrast between
the criminal guilt of the thief and the sacrificial
innocence of the Saviour: there is the contrast between the affecting penitence of the one felon and
the callous indifference of the other; and there is
the contrast between the two classes of people to
whom the story has particularly appealed. In a
casual kind of way, I have already instanced the
Marquis of Lossie as a representative of the one
class and the Countess of Huntingdon as a representative of the other. Let me now call two other
witnesses—one, like the Countess of Huntingdon,
from history, and the other, like the Marquis of
Lossie, from fiction. From history, as a type of
the one class, I cite Sydney Dobell: from fiction, as
a type of the other, I cite Tom Gibbons.

II

If ever a man wore the white flower of a blameless life, it was Sydney Dobell. His life-story is an
idyll of innocence. As soon as he was born, he was
'little angel-face,' and his delighted parents, wor-

shipping every trifle that those baby fingers touched, set themselves to guard their treasure from every contaminating influence. He never went to school or college or university; he was educated most carefully and most thoroughly by chosen tutors in the home; Mr. and Mrs. Dobell trembled lest, in contact with others, the slightest taint should sully the perfect purity of their boy's innocent mind. On every suitable occasion, the father would lead his boy to some quiet corner of the home, or to some lovely spot in the beautiful grounds, and would tell him the story of Jesus. And, laying his hand on Sydney's head and looking into his face, he invariably concluded the recital by saying how delightful it would be if *another* child should arise who would make it his supreme ambition to walk in the Saviour's footsteps, to live a holy, spotless and unselfish life, and to serve his fellowmen every day by doing his heavenly Father's will. The mother was no less earnest. 'Oh, how precious he was in my eyes!' she says. 'Surely never were prayers more devoutly uttered than for him; never child more sincerely devoted to God than was the treasure of my heart, my firstborn!'

Their effort to fill their boy's heart with a wondering reverence and supreme affection for all high and holy things was crowned with remarkable success. He gloried in the fields and the woods; he was never so happy as when climbing the hills and exploring the valleys of the English countryside.

He learned the lore of flowers and grasses and birds; his mind became steeped in the secrets of Nature's most delicious solitudes. To the unbounded delight of his parents, he made the New Testament his constant companion, and exhibited for it an unmistakable and growing affection. He would take it with him on his rambles, read it in silence in the leafy depths of the forest or seated among the cowslips on the banks of the stream. And then, on his return, he would carefully write out the passages that had most impressed him and note down the thoughts that had been suggested to his mind.

It was inevitable that a child so reared should be precocious, old-fashioned, abnormal. Moving so much in the society of his seniors, he matured quickly. He talked as grown-up people talked, and behaved pretty much as they do. When he was ten, a little girl of his own age visited the home, and Sydney fell violently in love with her. Five years afterwards—their minds remaining steadfast—the two became engaged; and, five years later still, at the age of twenty, they were married. When, in the full vigor of manhood, he began to move among men, he brought into the busy world the captivating innocence, the simple faith and the sunny sweetness of temper that had characterized his childhood, and all men capitulated to his charm. He was a striking and attractive figure, every way. He would have made a model for a Grecian sculptor. People turned on the street to take a second glance at him. He looked for all the world like some Castilian knight who had magically escaped from a volume of romance. He was tall, muscular and athletic, of graceful carriage and elastic stride. Revelling in the open air, his complexion was sunburnt and weather-beaten; whilst about his handsome face, with its deep blue eyes, there clustered a picturesque wealth of nut-brown hair. His fine features gave an irresistible impression of massiveness and princeliness; his whole appearance was arresting, magnetic and imposing.

Travel and intercourse with men swiftly broadened his mind and supplied, in large measure, the discipline that his severe isolation had denied him. The brooding thoughts of his long and lonely hours found expression in poesy; and, as soon as his poems were published, he had the world at his feet. Carlyle begged that he might be instantly supplied with every line that trickled from his magic pen. He made many distinguished friendships and kept them to the end. Browning and Tennyson, Mazzini and Ruskin, George Macdonald and Holman Hunt, Hugh Miller and Sir James Simpson, Thomas Carlyle and Charlotte Brontë were all of his circle; and, in each case, his friendship was highly prized. And, everywhere, the thing that fascinated everybody was the exquisite beauty of his simplicity, the bewitching charm of his unaffected innocence.

And the best of it was that, in the days of his

renown, he clung with unswerving tenacity to the things that, as a boy, he had learned to cherish. He still loved the green hills and the wooded valleys, and he travelled thousands of miles to feast his eyes on Europe's loveliest landscapes. He still treasured his New Testament and never moved without it. 'As a child,' he says, 'I learned the New Testament by heart, and I cannot unlearn the beauty of those sweet old Saxon phrases which I have loved so long. Full of the light that never was on sea or shore—the light of the holiest, happiest and best of recollections—I seem, in using them, to mingle a new element with earthly speech and relieve with their glory the dreary lifelessness of words.' His faith in the majestic simplicity of the everlasting gospel deepened and ripened with the years. He could not understand how any man, who had once realized the sweetness and power of the divine love, could forsake the pure fountain of his first faith. 'To me,' he wrote, 'there is no other name given under heaven among men whereby we must be saved. I shall never believe that the faith once delivered to the saints has grown obsolete till I see another faith delivered by the same hand to replace it. By God's help I will abide by Christ till Christ Himself shall release me. Till the veil of the temple is rent, I will worship there.'

The veil of the temple was rent early. He was only fifty. One lovely summer's evening, as his favorite rooks were winging their homeward way across the sky in front of his windows, his last breath was quietly drawn. The fading sunshine of a gorgeous August evening lay rich and deep upon the scene he loved so dearly. The arms of his wife were round him, and his hand was held by his mother. A happy smile played about his lips. The friends who gazed upon his face next day said that they had never seen anything so beautiful. He is buried in a lovely garden. The handsome granite cross, erected by his wife, which marks the spot in which he slumbers, is surrounded on every hand by pleasant lawns, evergreen shrubs, sweet-smelling herbs, well-kept flower beds, and all things fair and sweet. The air is choral with the hum of insects and the song of birds. It is a fitting resting-place for one of the most charming and blameless of Englishmen. Sydney Dobell was, as Professor James would say, 'a sky-blue soul,' with no cloud anywhere; his path shone more and more unto the perfect day.

But what has all this to do with the story of the Dying Thief? Much, every way. Sydney Dobell knew his New Testament from cover to cover. He learned it by heart, both in the original and in his native tongue. And, knowing the sacred volume through and through, one text stood out from all the rest. Some years before he died he gave instructions that it was to be inscribed upon his coffin. And it was. For there, on the coffin that was lowered into that garden-grave, was the dying thief's petition: *Lord, remember me when Thou comest into Thy Kingdom.* To his fellow men Sydney Dobell seemed to be the sweetest, sunniest and most stainless soul that any of them had known; yet when he passed into the presence of his Lord, he ranged himself with the thief on the cross, and, in a sincerity that sprang from his sense of inmost need, he made the malefactor's prayer his own. 'I must be saved as the dying thief was saved or not at all,' exclaimed the Countess of Huntingdon on her deathbed; and Sydney Dobell was of precisely the same mind.

III

By way of contrast, we turn to Tom Gibbons. Tom Gibbons is one of Peter B. Kyne's creations. He is the worst of the Three Bad Men in *The Three Godfathers.* The Three Bad Men have just raided the Wickenburg National Bank and are flying for their lives across the desert. There were, at first, four of them; but one was killed in the raid, and one of the three survivors is wounded. Out in the desert the three fugitives come upon a wagon beside a water-hole. The water-hole is dry; and the owner of the wagon, disappointed and alarmed, has lost his life in the course of a hopeless search for water. The dead man has left his young wife in the wagon, and, shortly after the arrival of the Three Bad Men, a baby is born. The three desperadoes pity the poor young mother; but they cannot help her; and she dies. But, in dying, she asks their names; makes them the godfathers of her baby; and solemnly commits him to their charge. They resolve that, at any sacrifice, they will save the baby's life.

As soon as the mother is dead, it occurs to them that she must have made some provision for the child; and they search the wagon. They find all that they need and—a Bible! Then they set out to fulfill their vow. How can it be done? How can the baby be carried across the desert and committed to some woman's arms? Tom Gibbons, the Worst Bad Man, feels that he can do a little; but he cannot hope to get the baby safely to civilization. Bill Kearney, the Wounded Bad Man, feels the same. Then it occurs to these two that if, for awhile, they do all that they can to save Bob Sangster, the Youngest Bad Man, *he* may be able to carry the baby to safety after *they* have fallen. Bob Sangster is little more than a boy; the bank-raid was his first adventure of the kind; the two old hands resolve to nurse his strength for the final endeavor. The Wounded Bad Man carries the baby as far as he can. But a time comes when he sinks in the desert, closes his eyes, and makes it clear that he will never stagger to his feet again. He asks for the Bible. The Youngest Bad Man gets it and reads to him. He selects the story of the Dying Thief. *'And he said unto Jesus, Lord, remember me when Thou comest into Thy Kingdom. And Jesus said unto him, Verily I say unto thee, To-day shalt thou be with Me in Paradise.'*

'That'll do, Bob!' exclaims the dying man; and, shortly after, they hear him murmuring to himself the prayers his mother taught him. And, when he passes, his mind is still pondering the passage he had just heard read. 'Don't—let—my—godson—die—between—two—thieves!' he says. 'And,' adds Mr. Kyne, 'some time during the night, the angels came and led Bill Kearney into Paradise.' Paradise! *'Thou shalt be with Me in Paradise!'*

The Worst Bad Man, Tom Gibbons, carries the baby as long as he can struggle on. Then he, too, sinks upon the sand. And, in the awful delirium of death, he cries again and again: *Lord, remember me when Thou comest into Thy Kingdom!* 'And perhaps,' says Mr. Kyne, 'perhaps there came back to him a message that only the Worst Bad Man could understand—the message of hope eternal sounding down the ages—*To-day thou shalt be with Me in Paradise!'* And, from his comrade's arms, the Youngest Bad Man takes the baby for whom one good woman and two bad men have died, and, after a desperate struggle, carries him to safety.

IV

'It makes my heart swell to think of it, my Lord!' says Mr. Graham, as he tells the dying Marquis the story of the Dying Thief.

'*I must be saved as he was or not at all!*' exclaims the aged Countess of Huntingdon.

'*That'll do!   That'll do!*' cry Mr. Kyne's desperadoes, as they listen to the touching record.

'*Give me,*' prayed Copernicus upon his deathbed, '*give me that grace of repentance and of faith which was vouchsafed, in his last hour, to the thief upon the cross!*'

'I range myself beside him and make his prayer my own,' says Sydney Dobell. 'I wish his words inscribed upon my coffin as the cry of my own heart. For,' he adds, '*to me there is no other name given among men whereby we must be saved!*'

And he—whoever he may be—who relies upon the mighty virtues of that Name, and learns to pray the malefactor's prayer, will never fail to hear within the secrecy of his soul the gracious and divine response: *Thou shalt be with Me!   With Me in Paradise!*

14

CHARLES G. FINNEY'S TEXT
1792–1875
Lawyer, revivalist, and president of Oberlin College.

Jeremiah 29:13

I

CHARLES GRANDISON FINNEY was a lawyer to his finger-tips. It was his law-books that made a Christian of him. In a sense of which Paul never dreamed, *'the law was his schoolmaster to lead him to Christ.'* When at the age of twenty-six, he entered the office of Mr. Benjamin Wright, a prominent attorney in Jefferson County, New York, he was, he assures us, as ignorant of religion as a heathen. He had not heard half a dozen sermons in his life, and had never felt the slightest interest in the matters with which the preachers dealt. But the law-books cured all that. The law-books opened his eyes. 'In studying law,' he says, 'I found the old authors frequently quoting the Scriptures, and referring especially to the Mosaic enactments as authority for many of the great principles of common law. This excited my curiosity so much that I went and purchased a Bible, the first I had ever owned; and whenever I found a reference by the law-authors to the Bible, I turned to the passage and consulted it in its connection. This led to my taking a deep interest in the Bible.'

From that time forth, the young student lived on his law-books and his Bible. The two classes of literature were always within reach. Sometimes the one was uppermost and sometimes the other. As long as the Bible appealed only to his legal and intellectual faculties, he allowed it to lie about his desk like any other book of reference. 'It never occurred to me,' he says, 'to be ashamed of reading it.' But, when the Bible began to strike a deeper note, and to awaken in his soul spiritual convictions and responses, a singular sensitiveness crept over him. 'I kept my Bible out of sight. If I was reading it when anybody came in, I would throw my law-books upon it.' And so the law-books and the Bible shared his heart between them. In the end, the Bible won. Little by little, the Bible took its place as the Supreme Assize, the Final Court of Appeal, the one august tribunal to which all questions were submitted. 'I felt myself shut up to my Bible,' he says.

The law-books had to take second place to the Bible; but they never sank below that. Finney was a lawyer to the end of the chapter. He thought as a solicitor thinks; he pleaded as a barrister pleads; he had merely accepted, as he himself put it, a retainer from the Lord Jesus Christ to plead *His* cause. It soon became clear that, if he had declined that retainer, and pursued his profession in the ordinary way, he would quickly have climbed to its highest places and won its most coveted prizes. His vigorous personality, his acute intellect and his persuasive oratory would have secured for him the

most dazzling distinctions that the courts and legis-
latures of his country could confer. Somebody
said that his preaching was 'logic on fire.' For this
reason he appealed, as no other man ever appealed,
to the legal mind. 'I have always been particularly
interested,' he said, towards the close of his life, 'in
the salvation of members of the legal profession. I
understood pretty well their habits of reading and
thinking. I have always found that when the gospel was properly presented, they were the most
accessible class; and, in proportion to their number,
more of them have been converted than of any
other class. I have often been impressed, in con-
versing with members of the legal profession, by the
manner in which they would consent to propositions
to which persons of ill-disciplined minds would have
objected.' 'It has often interested me to notice,' he
says again, 'that when lawyers have come to my
room, they were ready to submit to Christ the
moment that their difficulties were cleared up. Indeed, they take a more intelligent view of the plan
of salvation than any other class with whom I have
had to do.' Finney believed that the gospel was
pre-eminently reasonable. Unbelief, he argued, was
an intellectual absurdity, a prostration and a stulti-
fication of man's proudest and stateliest powers. He
saw an even loftier logic in Calvary than in Sinai.
And, appealing to the intelligence, as well as to the
conscience, of two continents, he gained, in an extraordinary way, the verdict that he sought.

II

No preacher was privileged to take a hand in the conversion of Charles Finney. It was his Bible that did it; and *one text* in particular. As soon as that Bible of his began to touch that deeper chord within his soul, he separated it from the law-books at the office, took it home, and began to read it in secret. It was no longer a book of *reference* but a book of *revelations.* 'Just at this point,' he says, 'the whole question of my personal salvation opened to my mind in a manner most marvellous at the time. I clearly saw the reality and fulness of the atonement of Christ. I saw that His work was a finished work —full and complete. And I saw that all that was necessary on my part was to get my own consent to give up my sins and accept the Saviour.'

Wanting in Him—Nothing! 'I saw that His work is a finished work, full and complete!'

Wanting in Me—My Own Consent! 'I saw that all that was necessary on my part was to get my own consent to give up my sins and accept the Saviour!'

It was on October 10, 1821—a day that he annually commemorated—that our young lawyer, with his keen, analytical mind, narrowed the issue down to this definite compass. It was early morning. He had been reading his Bible before starting for the office. And, now that the crucial question stood out so clearly, he resolved to settle it once for all. Just outside the village was a thick wood, choral with the song of birds and carpeted with wild flowers. Often on a summer's evening, or on a Sunday, he had sought its delicious seclusion. He resolved to go to it, instead of to the office, on this misty autumn morning. Penetrating the thickest part of the forest, he found a place where several giant trees had fallen across each other, leaving an open space between. He resolved to make this enclosed space the sanctuary of his soul. As he crept into it he vowed that he would never leave it until he had received the assurance of salvation. He knelt in prayer; but there came no answer to his frantic supplication. He heard a rustling among the leaves; he fancied that his devotions were observed; and he rose in confusion and dismay. Then, ashamed of his shame, he shouted at the top of his voice, declaring that he would not leave that woodland retreat unforgiven, though all the men on earth and all the devils in hell stood gaping around him. 'To think,' he said, 'that I should have been ashamed of being caught in the act of making my peace with my offended God! The wickedness of it appeared awful, infinite! It broke me down!' And, with that outbreak of contrition, the light suddenly dawned! Like a bolt from the blue, a passage of Scripture shot into his heart: *Ye shall seek Me and find Me when ye shall search for Me with all your heart!*

Ye shall seek Me!

Ye shall find Me!

When ye shall search with all your heart!

'I do not think,' he says, 'that I had ever read that passage, but I felt that it was the Word of God. I instantly seized hold of it with my whole heart. I was as conscious of trusting at that moment in the veracity of my God as I was of my own existence. "Lord," I cried, "I take Thee at Thy word! Thou knowest that I do search for Thee *with all my heart.* I have come to this place for that very purpose; and Thou hast promised that I shall find Thee!" That seemed to settle the whole question. I felt that I had performed my vow.'

He had sought!

He had found!

For he had searched for God with all his heart!

He walked back to the village and found that it was dinner-time; he had spent the whole morning in that leafy sanctuary! Devoting the afternoon to the office, he then went home. 'There was no fire, and no light, in the room; yet it appeared to be perfectly light. As I went in and shut the door, it seemed as if I met the Lord Jesus Christ face to face. He said nothing, but simply stood before me; and I fell down at His feet and poured out my soul to Him.' And there, in the evening, the work of the morning was consummated and crowned.

III

With all thine heart! 'The Spirit seemed,' he says, 'to lay stress on those four words: *with all thine heart.'* 'Ye shall seek Me and find Me when ye shall search for Me *with all thine heart!'*

With all thine heart! That is ever the stipulation of love. Love knows only one unpardonable sin: it is the sin of apathy. She will overlook any other defect, but she can never forgive a phlegmatic lover. She capitulates unconditionally to the whole-hearted. *With all thine heart!* She loves the lover whose passion is never daunted; the lover whose love is a fire burning in his bones; the lover who will not take No for an answer. She loves to be courted with ardor, persistence and intensity. And these three priceless qualities—ardor, persistence and intensity —were the outstanding characteristics of Charles G. Finney. They shone through his conversion and they flamed through the great heroic life that followed. *With all his heart* he believed; *with all his heart* he labored; and *with all his heart* he preached to countless thousands the everlasting gospel.

His intensity was the intensity of a great *fear*. He felt that his sins had intervened between him and his God, and that, unless he could get rid of them, there was the gravest possible danger that the estrangement might prove permanent. The thought filled him with unutterable alarm; he often closed his Bible with a shudder.

His intensity was the intensity of a great *faith*. 'O woman, great is thy faith!' said the Saviour to the Syro-Phoenician woman who would not be repulsed; and Finney's faith was modelled on hers. 'I will never leave this place,' he said, as he clambered over the fallen trees, 'I will never leave this place until I have received the assurance of salvation!' It was an echo of the faith that made Jacob a prince with God. 'I will not let Thee go,' he said to the angel that wrestled with him, 'except Thou bless me!' The kingdom of heaven suffereth violence and the violent take it by storm. That was the secret of Charles Finney's triumph.

His intensity was the intensity of a great *fervor*. He was borne down, as he himself puts it, with the weight of immortal souls; and he preached *with all his heart* in hope of saving them. 'He thunders and lightens,' says Dr. John Campbell, of Whitefield's Tabernacle, 'he thunders and lightens in a manner to shake the heart of any assembly, rousing the most apathetic and awing the most careless. At times his voice falters and his eyes become suffused with tears.' He made men feel that he was in deadly earnest, and that the things of which he spoke were the only things that mattered.

IV

A fiery spirit was Finney's. To the end of his long life he stated his case as an advocate states it; his logic was penetrating, pitiless, overwhelming; but it was *logic on fire*. He reasoned *with all his heart;* and his heart was hot.

A fiery spirit was his; and *fire burns!* It consumes, purges, devours. Whenever Finney preached, evil shrivelled up, withered, or slunk away in shame. After Finney visited a town, people were busy for days in restoring treasure to which they were not entitled. One man sent another a cheque for fifteen hundred pounds. 'If,' he wrote, 'it is right for a man to love his neighbor as himself, it was wrong for me to pocket this.' Another sent three hundred pounds. 'The transaction by which I acquired it was not quite honest,' he said. 'I have been examining the records of our criminal courts,' wrote a Rochester attorney to Mr. Finney, 'and I find that, whereas our city has increased threefold since your visit, there are not one-third as many prosecutions as there had been up to that time.' And so, as Whittier would say:

> . . . the flood of emotion, deep and strong,
> Troubled the land as it swept along,
> But left a result in holier lives.

Finney's missions were called revivals; but they were ethical revivals. Wickedness wilted like a weed in a flame. Finney was fiery; and *fire burns!*

And *fire hurts!* Finney's intensity often stung. As I turn the pages of his autobiography, I see him constantly subjected to violence and persecution. At one place, he is molested by an angry mob; at another, a gang of roughs have sworn to tar and feather him; at a third, the police discover a plot that aimed at his very life. Because of his friendship with Lloyd Garrison, the pioneer abolitionist, and of his sympathy with the cause of the slaves, his church was burned to the ground, the firemen refusing to extinguish the flames. He preached *with all his heart;* he was fiery; and *fire hurts!*

And *fire spreads!* I am arrested by an interesting coincidence. When Mr. Moody paid his first visit to England, Dr. Dale attended the meetings to ascertain, if he could, the secret of the evangelist's extraordinary power. 'His preaching,' wrote Dr. Dale, in recording his experience, 'his preaching had all the effect of Luther's; he exulted in the free grace of God. *His joy was contagious.* Men leaped out of darkness into light and lived a Christian life for ever afterwards.' Now, singularly, enough, Dr. Dale's predecessor at Carr's Lane—John Angell James—submitted Mr. Moody's predecessor—Charles G. Finney—to an identically similar investigation. And he came to an identically similar conclusion. The enormous crowds; the profound impression; the spiritual awakening; the ethical reformation; it was the *contagion of the preacher's joy!* Finney was fiery; and *fire spreads!*

V

As a young man, Finney walked out of his office declaring that he had received a retainer from the Lord Jesus Christ to plead *His* cause. He gained his verdict in the hearts of two great nations. His converts were countless. Dr. Charles Bush says that, in one year, the Churches of Rochester Presbytery

welcomed more than twelve hundred new members
as a result of his ministry. His books were read
with avidity at every fireside in England and
America. As Professor of Pastoral Theology at
Oberlin College, he impressed his character upon
all his students and infected them with his intense
and ardent spirit.

He worked *with all his heart* to the very, very
end. He was eighty-three. He still stood erect;
his fine figure inspired universal reverence; and his
life abounded in noble and gracious ministries. On
a beautiful Sunday evening in the summer of 1875,
he did not go to church. But, at sunset, he walked
with his wife to the gate to hear the music wafted
towards them from the open windows of the sanctuary. And then he went to bed—and to sleep. He
awoke in the presence of his Lord. *He had sought
Him and found Him, for he had searched with all
his heart.*

15

ROSALIE JOYCE'S TEXT

Character from *A Peep Behind the Scenes* by Mrs. O. F. Walton.

Matthew 18:11

I

As the lumbering old caravan crawled along the country road that lovely Sunday evening, the bells of the village church filled the balmy air with their sweetest music.

'Can't you hear the bells nicely now, Mammie?' said Rosalie.

'Yes,' said the poor woman, 'they sound just like the bells of our little church at home. I could almost cry when I hear them.'

On a broad open space close to the church, the caravan came to a halt. The bells ceased, and the sound of singing proceeded from the open doors. The service had begun.

'Mammie, dear,' said Rosalie, 'may I go and peep in at the church?'

Permission being granted, she hurried away. She peeped in, and she crept in. She had never been at a church service before.

'Where have you been all this time, Rosalie?' asked the anxious woman when at last the child returned.

Rosalie told of all that she had heard and seen.

'And he kept on saying your text, Mammie,' she said, 'the text on your picture there: *The Son of Man is come to seek and to save that which was lost!'*

The text on the picture! Yes, there it was! One wet Sunday afternoon, some time previously, a little old man with a rosy, good-tempered face had waded through a sea of mud from caravan to caravan distributing pictures among the travelling people of the shows. To Rosalie and her mother he gave a picture of the Good Shepherd carrying home his lost sheep. He helped them to hang it up on the wooden wall of their wandering home.

'There, ma'am,' he said, as he took his leave, 'you can look at that and think that the Good Shepherd is seeking you. He wants to find you, and take you up in His arms, and carry you home! And He won't mind the wounds it costs Him if you'll only let Him do it!'

Rosalie often wondered what it all meant. She read to herself the words under the picture again and again. And now, on her very first visit to a church, the minister had taken them for his text.

'The Son of Man is come!'

'The Son of Man is come to seek and to save!'

'The Son of Man is come to seek and to save that which was lost!'

II

It may be fancy, but, as I recall this incident from

A Peep Behind the Scenes, it seems to me that Rosalie's text stands inseparably associated with village greens. It was on a village green that the text was brought to the caravan; it was beside a village green that Rosalie heard the minister explain it. I once, as a little boy, heard Mr. Moody preaching on a village green, and his text that afternoon was Rosalie's text. Moreover, Mrs. Walton's book reminds me of George Eliot's. It was on a village green that Dinah Morris—in *Adam Bede*—preached her famous sermon. And her text, too, was Rosalie's text: *'The Son of Man is come to seek and to save that which was lost.'*

' "Lost!" cried Dinah, "lost!" And there was a great change in her voice and manner. She made a long pause, and the pause seemed to be filled by agitating thoughts that showed themselves in her features. At last it seemed as if, in her yearning desire to reclaim the lost sheep, she could not be satisfied by addressing her hearers as a body. She appealed first to one and then to another, beseeching them with tears to turn to God while there was yet time, painting to them the desolation of their souls, lost in sin, feeding on the husks of this miserable world, far away from God their Father; and then the love of the Saviour who was waiting and watching for them!'

'Lost!' said the picture in the caravan.

'Lost!' said the minister in the church.

'Lost!' cried Mr. Moody that Sunday afternoon.

'*Lost!*' exclaimed Dinah Morris on the Hayslope Green.

'*The Son of Man is come to seek and to save that which was lost!*'

III

'*The Son of Man is come to seek and to save that which was lost!*'

It is a string of monosyllables! The words are so simple that they awaken the soul of poor little Rosalie, catch the attention of the villagers lounging on the green, and enshrine themselves in the hearts of little children as they cluster round their mother's knee. And yet it is not so much with the simplicity of the passage as with its sublimity that I am impressed just now. We speak of the 'simple gospel' as though it had no heights unscaleable, no depths unfathomable, no lengths and breadths which human minds cannot discover and explore. We speak of the simplicity of such words as 'Jesus died for me,' and we forget that eternal mysteries lie hid, in every syllable of such a phrase, which angels cannot hymn nor archangels explain.

> Jesus came—and died for me!
>   Simple words; and yet expressing
> Depths of holy mystery,
>   Depths of wondrous love and blessing.

When the saintly John Fletcher of Madeley lay dying of a malady which he had contracted by unremitting attendance upon his fever-stricken people, he called upon his wife and maid servant to sing and shout of the vastness and splendor of the love of God. 'God is love!' he cried; 'sing of it, shout of it, both of you!' His wife quoted to him one of John Wesley's noblest translations. She knew how he loved the lines:

> Mercy's full power I soon shall prove,
> Loved with an everlasting love.

When, in the course of that bedside recital, she repeated the words:

> While Jesus' blood through earth and skies,
> Mercy—free, *boundless* mercy cries!

he caught at the thought that was most upon his heart; and, a little later, raising his hand and exclaiming 'Boundless, *boundless,* BOUNDLESS!' died. It is just that element of boundlessness that arrests me as I gaze with Rosalie upon the picture in the caravan and listen with her to the sermon in the village church.

IV

For who can stand before Rosalie's picture and contemplate Rosalie's text without being profoundly impressed by the boundlessness of the Saviour's *Personality?* *'The Son of Man!'* The title is full of suggestiveness. It is grand, dignified, sublime. He was a son of a man; but He was more. He was *the* son of a man; but He was more. He was a son of *Man;* but He was more. He was *the Son of Man.* What did it mean?

He stood, as Carlyle would say, in the centre of immensities, in the conflux of eternities; and, looking backwards, He saw what we rightly call the Fall of *Man.* And He remembered the words of promise and of hope that He Himself had spoken amid the sorrows of a sin-stricken Eden. Man as man had fallen, and to Man He had uttered that great word that the seed of the woman should bruise the serpent's head. And, ever since, *Man* had been looking with grief upon the long procession of its sons, but with eager expectancy for its *Son*—that sinless Son of a sinful race who was to bring deliverance, redemption and triumph over the coils of the serpent.

And at last, a voice is heard, saying, *'The Son of Man is come!'* And the world only failed to rejoice because it failed to see in that mystic title the greatness and the glory of its high significance. Christ was the Son of the Race. And the Race may well rejoice over her Son with joy unspeakable and full of glory. Christ was the Son of no empire, nation, kindred or tribe. The art galleries of the nations prove, with striking vividness, that each people has claimed Him as its own. And they have claimed Him rightly. The wide world was His Mother Country; Heaven itself His Fatherland; and the Race does well to hold its single Son in reverence and in love.

Some called Him the Son of Abraham: and it was true; but He was more. Some called Him the Son of David; and it was true; but He was more. Some called Him the Son of Mary; and it was true; but He was more. Those who called Him the Son of Abraham imposed upon Him a *racial* limitation; those who called Him the Son of David imposed upon Him a *kingly* limitation; those who called Him the Son of Mary imposed upon Him a *domestic* limitation. He shook Himself free from them all and cried: *'The Son of Man is come!'* Herein is boundlessness! Like His love, He 'passeth knowledge,' and, like the peace of God, He 'passeth all understanding.' 'Can you understand Jesus Christ?' someone asked of Daniel Webster one day, when the great statesman was surrounded by a group of literary acquaintances. 'No!' he replied, 'I would be ashamed to acknowledge Him as my Saviour if I could understand Him. I need a superhuman Saviour—one so great and glorious that I cannot comprehend Him!'

V

And who can stand before Rosalie's picture and contemplate Rosalie's text without being amazed at the boundlessness of the Saviour's *Constituency?* *'That which is lost!'* It seemed an awful task, even to His disciples as He said it, but let the fancy contrast *His* vision with *theirs.* *They* saw a little world lapped from end to end by the blue waters of the Mediterranean. But *He* saw hosts of men, tier above tier, clime beyond clime, nations and empires and continents all unsuspected and unknown, generation above generation, century beyond century, age after age!

'That which is lost!' His constituency was subject to no bounds or limitations. He knew no masses and no classes, no old and no young, no high and no low, no rich and no poor. Wherever in the wide, wide world *'that which is lost'* existed, the Son of Man came to seek and to save it. He came to save the lost monarch, with his glittering diadem and ermine robes, lost in his fatal pride and independence. He came to save the lost ne'er-do-well, tramping aimlessly, hopelessly, grimly, doggedly, through tussock and scrub, over our silent inland hills—lost in carelessness and despair. He came to save the lost son in his midnight carousals and debauchery; He came to save the lost daughter, shuddering in her dreadful humiliation and shame. He came to save the lost loiterer lounging at the corners of our city streets; the lost sailor on the wild high seas; the lost scholar dazed amid the splendid problems of his theories and philosophies; the lost Pharisee, who, faultily faultless and icily regular, is too far lost to know that he is lost; and He came to save the lost ordinary man—lost *you,* lost *me!*

He came to save the lost. They may be lost sadly and strikingly, like the younger and favorite of *two* sons—a loss that constitutes a great and aching void which nothing else can fill. They may be lost less noticeably, less painfully, like one piece of silver out of *ten*. Or they may be lost like one sheep out of a *hundred,* which none but One would ever miss. No matter who, no matter how, no matter when, no matter where; *'that which is lost'* is His special care and charge. It is His boundless constituency.

I really think that the best exposition of Rosalie's text is Rosalie's own. Rosalie was indulging one day in a confidential chat with a boy named Jinx from another caravan. The conversation naturally turned to the picture.

'You see, Jinx,' said the wise little Rosalie, 'there are only three kinds of sheep—the ninety and nine who never went astray; the sheep that the Shepherd has found and is bringing back on His shoulders; and the sheep that are lost.'

'Is that all the kinds?' asked poor Jinx.

'Yes; why?'

'Well,' replied Jinx, 'you see I can't be one of the ninety and nine, because I've done lots of bad things in my life. I've got into tempers, and I've sworn, and I've done heaps of wicked things; so *that's* out of the question. And I can't be a *found* sheep, because I don't love the Good Shepherd—I never think about Him at all; so I must be a *lost* sheep. That's a dreadful thing to be, isn't it?'

'Yes, very bad,' said Rosalie, sympathetically; and then, with a sudden flash of illumination, 'but

if you're a *lost* sheep, you're the very sheep that
Jesus came to save, for *"the Son of Man is come to
seek and to save that which was lost!"* '

I do not know what the minister said about the
text that night in the village church; but I am sure
that he said nothing better than *that*.

VI

And who can stand before Rosalie's picture and
contemplate Rosalie's text without being lost in
admiration at the boundlessness of the Saviour's
Programme? '*To seek and to save!*' The accent of
certainty that rings through the words is as melodious as the bells that Rosalie heard that Sunday
evening. He came, not to seek to save, but to seek
and to save. He came, not to attempt, but to do;
not to try, but to triumph!

That was always the occupation of Jesus—always
seeking the lost. You will find the world's heroes
where the banquets are the gayest, where the flowers
are the fairest, where the plaudits ring the loudest,
where the songs rise the sweetest, where music
swells the most voluptuously. You will find Jesus
by the well with a guilty woman; you will find Him
at the gates of Nain with a widow doubly crushed;
you will find Him at the tomb with two weeping
sisters; you will find Him alone with a maiden
wrapped in the icy slumber of death; you will find
Him where passion sweeps the fiercest, where the
anguish is the keenest, where the heartbreak is the

saddest, where the loss is the heaviest, where the tears are the bitterest, for *the Son of Man is come to seek and to save that which was lost.*

He is always *seeking.* That is what Francis Thompson, with such rare insight and such real felicity, has sought to convey to us in his *Hound of Heaven.*

> I fled Him down the nights and down the days;
>   I fled Him down the arches of the years;
> I fled Him, down the labyrinthine ways
>   Of my own mind; and in the midst of tears
> I hid from Him, and under running laughter
>   Up vistaed hopes, I sped;
>   And shot, precipitated
> Adown Titanic glooms of chasmed fears,
> From these strong Feet that followed, followed after,
>   But with unhurrying chase
>   And unperturbed pace,
> Deliberate speed, majestic instancy,
>   They beat—and a Voice beat
>   More instant than the Feet—
> 'Lo, all things fly thee as thou fliest Me.'

As long as we evade Him, all real happiness evades us.

For, *seeking,* He comes to *save.* And here He stands absolutely alone, solitary, unique. Herein His ministry ineffably supersedes and transcends all the ministries of men. Supposing all others who are seeking to save humanity with well-contrived schemes of social salvation ever reach their goal; supposing philanthropy, altruism and socialism ever banish from the earth the hideous forms of squalor, poverty, want, and even drink and vice; supposing at last every home is prettily and comfortably housed, environed by a smiling world—what then? If the hearts within those fair homes are still Christless, still unregenerate, you have only driven their misery further in. You have healed the skin over the wound whilst the flesh is yet unclean. You have painted and varnished rotten wood. For such a hollow parody on salvation the world will not long thank you, but, in the first hungry pangs of its disappointment and remorse, will turn again and rend you.

> Give the winds a mighty voice,
>   Jesus saves, Jesus saves!
> Let all nations now rejoice,
>   Jesus saves, Jesus saves!
> Shout salvation full and free
>   To every strand that ocean laves,
> This our song of victory—
>   Jesus SAVES, Jesus SAVES!

VII

'Mammie, dear,' said Rosalie, one day, 'shall we tell Him?'

'Tell Him what, my dear?'

'Just tell Him that you and me want seeking and finding!'

'I don't know, Rosalie; you can try!'

'Please, Good Shepherd,' prayed Rosalie, 'come

and seek me and Mammie, and find us very quick and carry us very safe—like the lamb in the picture!'

I do not know what petitions the minister offered in the village church that Sunday night; but I am sure he offered no prayer more acceptable to heaven than *that!*

16

JOHN WILLIAMS' TEXT
1796–1841
British missionary to the South Pacific islands.

John 8:36

I

THE boys who were born in the closing years of the eighteenth century were swept off their feet by the audacious exploits of Captain Cook. That intrepid navigator had fired their fancies with the vision of a new world. His adventurous voyages, his sensational discoveries and his tragic death were the talk of the time. In every playground in England, schoolboys were dreaming feverish day-dreams of coral reefs and cannibal islands away in southern seas. William Carey was one of those boys; John Williams was another. 'If I had the means,' said Carey, 'I would go to the South Seas and commence a mission at Otaheiti.' He changed his mind, however, and went to India, leaving to John Williams that vast expanse of sea and land that Captain Cook had so recently explored.

John Williams was just the man for the moment; he seemed to have been built on purpose. Sailing in the wake of our greatest navigator, he caught so perfectly the spirit of his illustrious predecessor that he was able to continue and complete his work. He discovered Raratonga, an island that had eluded the sharp eyes and tireless researches of Captain

Cook and his companions. In boats that he himself
had built, he sailed 'from island unto island at the
gateways of the day.' As soon as he had established
a footing on one group, he pushed on to another.
When the authorities in England questioned his wisdom in roving like a viking round the Pacific, he
told them frankly that no other programme would
appease his conscience. 'A missionary,' he wrote,
'was never designed by Jesus Christ to gather a congregation of a hundred or two natives, and sit down
at his ease, as contented as if every sinner were converted, while thousands around him, and but a few
miles off, are eating each other's flesh and drinking
each other's blood, living and dying without the
gospel. For my own part, *I cannot content myself
within the narrow limits of a single reef.'* If, he
said, the committee discountenanced his ship-building and denied him further facilities for navigation,
he would a thousand times rather be stationed on
a continent, 'for there, if you cannot ride, you can
walk; but to these scattered islands only a ship can
carry you.' He was always looking for new worlds
to conquer. And he conquered them. Take Raratonga for example. He discovered it in 1823 and
commenced evangelistic activities at once. He planted
several mission stations, committing them to the care
of his native workers. Therein, his son thinks, lay
the genius of his statesmanship; he knew how to
make missionaries of his converts. Five years later,
he had two of his fellow-countrymen in residence

on the island superintending all the operations there. Six years later still, he is able to report that Raratonga has been completely evangelized; its idols have all been destroyed by their former worshippers; three spacious and substantial churches have been erected; the people have the Word of God in their own language, and, he adds, 'I am not aware that there is a house in the island where family worship is not observed every morning and every evening.' He is delighted at the way in which civilization and commerce have followed in the train of Christianity; and, on almost the last day of his life, he completed arrangements for the establishment on the island of a college in which suitable young men were to be thoroughly educated, and taught the useful arts, with a view to their becoming the leaders and instructors of their own people. He was, as Dr. Campbell finely said, 'a man who has achieved for himself a deathless fame, and one concerning whom generations to come will feel a laudable and reverent curiosity.'

II

It was on the first Sunday of the New Year that Mr. Spurgeon was suddenly arrested by the power of the gospel. It was on the first Sunday of the New Year that, no less startlingly, John Williams was enlisted in the Saviour's service. And in each case it was a text that did it. Mr. Spurgeon liked to tell the story of John Williams' conversion, because, in some respects, it so closely resembled his own. It was on a sharp, frosty evening—the evening of Sunday, January 3, 1819. Soon after dusk, a cold sleet had fallen; but the weather had cleared, and throngs of people, hurrying this way and that, were responding to the melodious invitation of the bells. On her way to church, Mrs. Tonkin, in passing along City Road, was struck by the appearance of a tall young fellow who seemed to be lounging aimlessly at the street corner. He was a lad of about eighteen, stalwart and sinewy, already giving promise of vast physical energy. As the lamplight fell upon his fine open countenance, she turned and fastened upon him a second and more penetrating glance. Something about him seemed familiar; where had she seen that face before? To be sure! he was one of her husband's apprentices; she remembered noticing him in the workshop. She paused, and then went back to him. He explained that he had made an appointment with some friends to meet at this corner and to spend the evening at a tavern at Highbury. His companions, however, had failed to put in an appearance; and he was feeling vexed and disappointed. 'My course of life at this period,' he wrote afterwards, 'was very wicked though not flagrantly immoral. I was regardless of the Sabbath; a lover of pleasure more than a lover of God; I often scoffed at the name of Christ and His religion; and I totally neglected those things which alone can afford solid consolation.' Mrs.

Tonkin urged him to accompany her to Moorfields Tabernacle. With a little persuasion, he consented.

Twenty-four years afterwards, on the occasion of his visit to England, he stood in the pulpit of that very building and told a crowded congregation of that youthful yet momentous experience of his. 'I have in my view at the present moment,' he said, 'the door by which I entered; I have all the circumstances of that important era in my history vividly impressed upon my mind; I have in my eye at this instant the particular spot on which I took my seat. I have also a distinct impression of the powerful sermon that was that evening preached by the excellent Mr. East. That good man took for his text that night one of the most impressive questions of inspired writ: *What shall it profit a man if he shall gain the whole world and lose his own soul?* God was pleased in His own gracious providence to influence my mind so powerfully that I forsook all my worldly companions and became a teacher in the Sabbath-school connected with this place. Many a Sabbath afterwards did I sit upon the form now in my sight with my class, and impart that knowledge to *them* which God in His gracious goodness had given to *me.*'

It was thus that the supreme issues of human life —the world and the soul—*his* world and *his* soul— were suddenly presented for his contemplation.

The world: his world!
The soul: his soul!

To gain the world: to lose his soul!

What shall it profit a man if he shall gain the whole world and lose his own soul?

John Williams resolved that Sunday night that his immortal soul should on no account be lost; and he resolved to win a larger world than the paltry world on which, up to that moment, his heart had been set.

III

I do not know—I should like to know—how Mr. East dealt that evening with this old, old question. It must have been in some new and striking way. Perhaps he took it to pieces. It sometimes happens that you get so used to a thing as a whole that you only realize the wonder of its composition when its component parts are all spread out before you. A gun, a clock, a microscope looks commonplace; but, let a skilful mechanic take it to pieces before your eyes, and you stand astonished at its delicate settings and beautiful adjustments. It may be that Mr. East did something of the kind that night. He may have talked for awhile on the wisdom of weighing the issues of life and of computing its profit—or loss. He may have discussed the unutterable value of the individual soul. He may have commented eloquently on the conquest of the world. I have sometimes fancied that a sermon could be preached on that fragment alone. To say nothing of the loss of the soul, *what shall it profit a man if he shall gain the whole world?*

It all depends. A man might gain an inconsiderable fraction of the world and be immensely profited, or, on the other hand, he might gain the whole world without being profited at all. As I say, it all depends. And it depends, not upon the world, but upon himself. Everybody knows the Eastern story of the man who, becoming extremely rich, built for himself a magnificent palace. He lived in it with perfect satisfaction until somebody told him that no palace was complete unless a roc's egg hung suspended from its roof. The unhappy man thereupon set out to find a roc's egg, and, always unsuccessful in his search, died in his mortification and discontent. Marshal Soult and the Duke of Wellington were one day inspecting Canova's statue of Napoleon, a statue which represents the emperor as the conqueror of the world. The globe is in his hand. Turning to the Duke, Soult remarked that it was very odd that a sculptor who understood so perfectly the science of proportion should have made the globe so extremely small. 'Ah,' replied the Duke, 'but *England was not in it!*' It was the story of the roc's egg over again. Our capacity for satisfaction depends, not on the splendor of our conquests, but on ourselves. A man may win the whole world, and, so far from being profited, may simply weep that there are no more worlds to conquer.

IV

If he gain the whole world!

If he lose his own soul!
The whole world! His own soul!
Neither is a negligible quantity. The man who
lives for *the whole world* and neglects *his own soul*
is a *Materialist;* the man who lives for *his own soul*
and neglects *the whole world* is a *Monk;* and neither
the *Materialist* nor the *Monk* represents the ideal of
perfect manhood.

To gain the whole world! A recent work of fiction tells us that, on the Corniche road, near to the
little village of Eze, where the splash of the Mediterranean waves is the only sound heard, you may see
an old tombstone with this strange inscription:
'Here lies *the soul* of Count Louis Esterfield.' Many
travellers had passed by during long years and read
it and wondered, repeating the words with puzzled
minds. Some laughed lightly, and others looked
grave, until at last came a man who having read
the epitaph, sat down beside the stone to ponder it.
After a while, he began to dig, and, working pa-
tiently for some time, he came upon a box made of
metal, and filled with jewels and gold. Among
them lay a paper on which was written: 'You are
my heir; to you I bequeath this wealth, for you
alone have understood me. In this box is *my soul!'*
An identically similar story occurs in the introduc-
tion to *Gil Blas.* In each case there is the sad,
despairing cry of a man who has gained his *whole*
world and lost *his own soul.* It is the misery of
the Materialist.

And the misery of the Monk is scarcely less pitiful. In his concern for *his own soul* he turns back upon *the whole world.* Luther did. 'I was indeed a pious monk,' he writes to Duke George of Saxony, 'and followed the rules of my order more strictly than I can express. If ever monk could obtain heaven by his monkish works, I should certainly have been entitled to it. Of this all the friars who have known me can testify. If it had continued much longer, I should have carried my mortification even to death, by means of my vigils, prayers, readings and other cloistral labors.' Happily, Luther remembers the world—the whole world— the world that God so loved—the world for which Christ died. And, remembering *the whole world,* he set out from his convent cell to win it; and he won it in a way that made his *soul* more than ever *his own.*

V

So did John Williams. For, that New Year's Sunday evening at Moorfields Tabernacle, he suddenly acquired a new view of the value of *his own soul* and a new view of the value of *the whole world.* The value of his soul impressed him immediately; the value of the world impressed him no less profoundly.

The whole world!
God so loved the world!
Go ye into all the world!

The visions that had fired his fancy as he pored over the stirring pages of Captain Cook rushed back upon his mind. 'If I had the means,' said William Carey, as he read *Cook's Voyages*, 'if I had the means, I would go to the South Seas and commence a mission at Otaheiti.' Carey went to India; but Williams went to Otaheiti. And, stranded there, he felt his utter helplessness. The world—even Cook's world—seemed wonderfully wide. 'If,' he wrote to a friend, 'if only I had a ship, I would visit every island in the Pacific and leave teachers on each one to direct the feet of the heathen to happiness and heaven.' At last he could endure his world-hunger no longer. Totally ignorant of the arts of ship-building, and entirely destitute of the necessary tools, he actually built a ship—the *Messenger of Peace*—a little vessel of seventy tons burthen. It was, as somebody said, the evidence no less of his fervid piety than of his matchless skill. The committee in England censured him for doing it; but he could not help it. 'The first sermon I ever preached in the native language,' he says, 'was from the text: *This is a faithful saying, and worthy of all acceptation, that Christ Jesus came into the world to save sinners.* I love that doctrine; and I am resolved never to preach a sermon in any language unless salvation through the blood of Christ is its sum and substance. It is a truth worth carrying to the whole world!'

The whole world!

God so loved the world!
Go ye into all the world!
His own soul! The whole world!

He won them both! In November, 1839, he sailed for Erromanga, an island that he had never visited before. *'The approaching week,'* he wrote in his diary, *'is to me the most important of my life.'* It was. The last entry in that journal reads: *'The results of this day will be—'* The sentence was never finished. For, that day, the natives of Erromanga slew him with their clubs. He was only forty-three. But he had held true to the great decision that he made at Moorfields Tabernacle as a boy. His *soul* was all *his own;* and he had bravely done his part towards the winning of *the whole wide world.*

17

W. M. Thackeray's Text

1811–1863

English novelist and author of *Vanity Fair.*

Psalm 37:25

I

'That text is worth a million pounds!' exclaimed Goldsmith's Vicar of Wakefield. Thackeray thought so too. He never actually put a price upon it, but he made it perfectly clear that he regarded it as invaluable. Every reader of *The Newcomes* knows Thackeray's text. Colonel Newcome is Thackeray's dream-man, his vision splendid, his beckoning ideal. It is because Thackeray took such pains to weave into the character of Thomas Newcome the simplicities and sublimities of his own faith that the Colonel has taken his place as the Grand Old Man of English fiction. He is, as somebody has said, the typical gentleman, perfect in all points and parts; never once insipid or dull; and, as we watch him grow old, we feel for him the affectionate solicitude that we cherish for a dear relation or an honored friend. He never seems more noble than when he stands, unconquered, amidst the calamities that overwhelm him at the last. In age and feebleness he is doomed to witness the shipwreck of his fortunes. Night falls upon him, not serene and starlit, but with black storm and raging tempest. Yet, in the darkest hour that ever closes round him, he stands, with spirit unbroken and faith unruffled, resting serenely in the shelter of a psalm.

In his poverty—a poverty in which there is no tinge of shame—he sits among the black-coated pensioners of the Hospital of Grey Friars. But with grateful heart and shining face he sets his seal to the testimony that he reads in the book that lies open on his knee. *The steps of a good man are ordered by the Lord. Though he fall, he shall not be utterly cast down: for the Lord upholdeth him with His hand. I have been young and now am old, yet have I not seen the righteous forsaken, nor his seed begging bread.* 'His dear old head,' says Arthur Pendennis, who, horrified at seeing him there, speedily effected his deliverance, 'his dear old head was bent down over the book, but there was no mistaking him. He wore the black gown of the pensioners; but his Order of the Bath was on his breast.' It seemed to Arthur an irony that the steps of this good man had been ordered of the Lord—to an almshouse! Impatient to reach his old friend, he at length succeeded in doing so. He found him in a little room which, though severely plain, was neat and comfortable; and, on the table, which was laid for tea, was the old man's Bible, with his spectacles beside it.

'Don't be agitated, Arthur, my boy,' exclaimed the old man soothingly. 'I am very happy. I have good quarters, good food, good light, good fire and

good friends. Blessed be God, my dear, kind young
friend, I am as happy as the day is long!'

Arthur thought, he tells us, of the Psalm that he
had heard the old man singing. *I have been young
and now am old, yet have I not seen the righteous
forsaken nor his seed begging bread.* He stepped
to the table and turned the pages of the old man's
Bible till he found it. The Colonel rose, laid a kind,
trembling hand upon Arthur's shoulder, and, with a
smile, bent over the volume. And who, Arthur
asks, could behold that smile without adoring the
grace that had achieved so notable and beautiful a
triumph?

II

But, in admiring Colonel Newcome, we must not
lose sight of Thackeray. We are too prone
to extol the creation and forget the creator. In
giving us this heroic and impressive picture of
Colonel Newcome, Thackeray was simply painting
a wonderfully revealing portrait of his own soul.
At least, he was painting a portrait of his own soul
as he would have liked his soul to be. You may
judge a man by his ideals; and Colonel Newcome
is Thackeray's. Thackeray brought Colonel Newcome into existence that, at his feet, we might all
learn to be trustful and brave. 'I like to think,'
the novelist once said, 'that my books have been
written by a God-loving man. Their morality—
the vanity of everything but love and goodness—

is but a reflection of the teaching of our Lord.' When Thackeray knew that his end was near, he was visited by an intimate friend—Mr. Synge—who was leaving England for some years.

'I want to tell you,' said Thackeray, 'that I shall never see you again. I feel that I am doomed. I know that this will grieve you; but look in that book, and you will find something that, I am sure, will please and comfort you.'

The 'something' was a written prayer in which he prayed that he might never write a word inconsistent with the love of God or the love of man; that he might never propagate his own prejudices or pander to those of others; that he might always speak the truth with his pen, and that he might never be actuated by love of greed. 'And I particularly remember,' Mr. Synge tells us, 'that the prayer wound up with the words: *For the sake of Jesus Christ our Lord.*' It was in the spirit of that prayer, and in answer to it, that Colonel Newcome's name appeared upon the pages of English literature.

It is eminently characteristic of Thackeray that it is from the Bible that, in the day of his calamity, old Colonel Newcome derives courage and hope. In all Thackeray's books that principle holds true. Whenever any of the characters find themselves faced by some stupendous crisis—a crisis of temporal disaster or a crisis of spiritual despair—it is invariably from the inspired pages of Scripture that

there comes the word of pardon or direction or
cheer. 'It would be easy,' as Sir Alfred Dale, the
late Vice-Chancellor of Leeds University, has finely
said, 'it would be easy to find a score of passages
in which Thackeray caught his inspiration from
gospel or from psalm. But there is one passage in
which he reveals himself unconsciously; and un-
conscious revelations are the surest. You remember the story of George Warrington in *Pendennis*
—the young man who has made shipwreck, and has
to atone for a single act of folly by a life without
ambition, without love, and almost without hope.
He is left to face it all alone, alone with the flowers
that recall the vision of joy that has come and
passed him by, and with the Bible that a grateful
mother has left as a parting gift; the fading flowers
and the unfading book; alone with them, alone with
the night. "And," Thackeray adds, "the morning
found him still reading in its awful pages, in which
so many stricken hearts, in which so many tender
and faithful souls have found comfort under
calamity and refuge and hope in affliction." '

Comfort under calamity!
Refuge and hope in affliction!

The words sum up with perfect accuracy the situation in which old Colonel Newcome found himself when the text came to his aid at Grey Friars!

*I have been young and now am old, yet have I
not seen the righteous forsaken nor his seed begging
bread.*

III

Now in my own copy of *The Newcomes* there is an introductory essay on Thackeray and his work. In the course of his critique, the writer compares Thackeray, first with Oliver Goldsmith and then with Sir Walter Scott. For my present purpose the comparison is extremely pertinent. For both Goldsmith and Scott knew the value of the words that so comforted the old Colonel.

I have been young and now am old, yet have I not seen the righteous forsaken nor his seed begging bread.

Thackeray, because of his reverent affection for the words, made them *Colonel Newcome's* text.

Goldsmith, because of his reverent affection for the words, made them the *Vicar of Wakefield's* text.

Sir Walter Scott, because of his reverent affection for the words, made them *Jeanie Deans'* text.

Like Colonel Newcome, the Vicar of Wakefield has sustained the shipwreck of his fortune. 'Out of fourteen thousand pounds,' he says, 'we had but four hundred remaining. My chief attention, therefore, was to bring down the pride of my family to their circumstances; for I well knew that aspiring beggary is wretchedness itself. As my oldest son was bred a scholar, I determined to send him to town, where his abilities might contribute to our support and his own. The separation of friends and families is, perhaps, one of the most distressful circumstances attendant on penury. The day soon arrived on which we were to disperse for the first time. My son, after taking leave of his mother and the rest, who mingled their tears with their kisses, came to ask a blessing from me. This I gave him from my heart, for, added to five guineas, this was all the patrimony I had now to bestow.

'You are going, my boy,' cried I, 'to London on foot. Take from me this staff, and take, too, this book; it will be your comfort on the way. These two lines in it are worth a million: *I have been young and now am old, yet have I not seen the righteous forsaken nor his seed begging bread.* Let this be your consolation as you travel on.'

I have often wondered how that paragraph found its way into *The Vicar of Wakefield.* No other English classic was penned under such squalid and degrading conditions as those which marked the production of Goldsmith's masterpiece. Dr. Johnson has made the episode historic. 'I received one morning,' he says, 'a message from poor Goldsmith that he was in great distress, and, as it was not in his power to come to me, he begged that I would come to him as soon as possible. I sent him a guinea and promised to come to him directly. I accordingly went as soon as I was dressed and found that, his rent being sadly in arrear, his landlady had placed him under arrest. I asked him to be calm and began to talk to him of the means by which he might be extricated. He then told me that he had a novel ready for the press which he produced. I looked into it and saw its merits; told the landlady I should soon return; and, having gone to the bookseller, sold it for sixty pounds.' That novel was *The Vicar of Wakefield!*

And here, embedded in that novel, is the text! When in his narrow attic, Goldsmith penned that paragraph about the text, was he recalling some such experience that befell himself on the day on which he left his father's home? His father, like the Vicar of Wakefield, was a country minister in reduced circumstances. He himself had left home in much the same way as George Primrose in the story. Did Oliver Goldsmith's father send him out into the world with that text, telling him that it was 'worth a million'? Did Goldsmith ponder it in his poverty? And did the text rush back upon his mind when Dr. Johnson returned from the bookseller's with the sixty golden coins? I cannot say for certain; but all the circumstances of the case point in that direction.

So much for Oliver Goldsmith; we must turn to Sir Walter Scott. And even Sir Walter Scott never wrote a tenderer idyll of Scottish life than that which we all cherish in *The Heart of Midlothian.* Jeanie Deans has made up her mind to tramp all the way from Edinburgh to London to plead with the King and Queen for the life of Effie, her sister. It happens that, at the moment of her projected departure, her father, old David Deans, and her lover,

Reuben Butler, are in circumstances of urgent necessity and distress. Effie languishes in a felon's cell. It breaks her heart to leave them all in such a plight; yet an appeal to the King and Queen seems to her the only way of deliverance. Before setting out on her long journey she calls on her lover to say good-bye. She asks for some papers, and, whilst he is away getting them, she hurriedly marks with his kylevine pen a passage in his Bible.

'I have marked a scripture that will be useful to us baith,' she told him a few moments afterwards, 'and ye must take the trouble, Reuben, to write out the words and send them to my father.'

What words were they? As soon as Jeanie had gone, Sir Walter tells us, Butler flew to the Bible—the last book she had touched—and pored eagerly over the text that she had underlined. *I have been young and now am old, yet have I not seen the righteous forsaken nor his seed begging bread.* Butler read the words again and again, and, as he did so, made it the supreme object of his ambition to attain to Jeanie's devout firmness and noble confidence.

IV

Now I have cited these pages from the classics, not because of their association with Colonel Newcome, the Vicar of Wakefield and Jeanie Deans, but because of their association with Thackeray, Goldsmith and Scott. The text must have meant something to Thackeray or he would never have made it Colonel Newcome's text; it must have meant something to Sir Walter Scott or he would never have made it Jeanie Deans' text; it must have meant something to Oliver Goldsmith or he would never have made the Vicar of Wakefield tell his son that the words were worth a million pounds.

But, after all, I could easily have dispensed with fiction. I could have called two other witnesses. For everybody who has read his *Last Journals* knows how often David Livingstone pillowed his fevered head on the thirty-seventh Psalm. As he made his way along those interminable slave-tracks, littered with the bones of the victims who had fallen; as he tossed in his delirium among the swamps and bogs of the watershed; as he faced death at the hands of hostile and infuriated savages; and as he endured untold agonies inflicted upon him by poisonous insects, venomous reptiles and wild beasts, he found one ceaseless fountain of inspiration and comfort. He would never be forsaken! He would never lack bread! *I have been young and now am old, yet have I not seen the righteous forsaken nor his seed begging bread.*

My other witness would have been a Covenanter, and one of the noblest of the Covenanters. Robert Baillie of Jerviswoode—the 'Algernon Sydney of Scotland'—was the great-grandson of John Knox. 'You have men of noble spirit in Scotland,' wrote Dr. John Owen, 'but Mr. Baillie of Jerviswoode

possesses the greatest abilities I ever met with.' He
was publicly hanged at the Market Cross of Edinburgh on Christmas Eve, 1684; his body was submitted to every indignity; and his property was con-
fiscated and forfeited to the Crown. Before being
led to the scaffold, he sent for his son and told him
that the bitterest ingredient in his anguish was the
fact that he was being compelled to leave his family
penniless. 'But,' he added, 'God's promises are sure,
and I am confident that the testimony of David will
be verified: *I have been young and now am old, yet
have I not seen the righteous forsaken nor his seed
begging bread.'*

V

Thackeray was a tremendous believer in the
Fatherly love of God. He had implicit and unwav-
ering confidence in the sheltering and protecting care
that God is able to exercise—*for the sake of Jesus
Christ our Lord.* 'I particularly noticed,' says Mr.
Synge, 'that he said *for the sake of Jesus Christ our
Lord.'* He thought it the loveliest thing in religion
that God allows Himself to be called Our Father—
Our Father *for the sake of Jesus Christ our Lord.*

Dr. John Brown tells how, one beautiful Sunday
evening, Thackeray went for a walk with two
friends in one of the most charming suburbs of
Edinburgh. The sky was a sea of glory: the hills
lay bathed in amethystine splendor: it was such a
sunset as one never forgets. 'The north-west end

of Corstorphine Hill, with its trees and rocks, lay in the heart of this pure radiance, and there a wooden crane, used in the granary below, was so placed as to assume the figure of a cross. There it was, unmistakably lifted up against the crystalline sky. All three gazed at it silently. Suddenly Thackeray gave utterance, in a gentle and tremulous voice, to what all were feeling. "Calvary!" he said, "Calvary!" The friends walked on in silence and then turned to other things. But all that evening Thackeray was very gentle and serious, speaking, as he seldom did, of divine things—of death, of sin, of eternity and of salvation—expressing his simple faith in God and in his Saviour.'

The Cross! Calvary!

Death! Sin! Salvation! Eternity!

The Fatherly Love of God—for the sake of Jesus Christ our Lord.

I have been young and now am old, yet have I not seen the righteous forsaken nor his seed begging bread.

Such a faith, Goldsmith says, is worth a million pounds; and certainly nobody who has once made it his own would dream of parting with it at that price.

18

COUNTESS OF HUNTINGDON'S TEXT

1707–1791

Aristocratic supporter of the English evangelical revival.

1 Corinthians 3:11

I

THE Countess of Huntingdon stands absolutely alone in history. Her extraordinary achievement is without precedent and without parallel; in all our annals there is no record that we can compare with hers. Since the world began, no one person of either sex has done for any nation what she did for ours. It is the unique distinction of her long and illustrious career that, without thrusting herself into prominence or compromising in the slightest degree the instinctive delicacy of her sex, she compelled every man in England, from the king upon his throne to the ploughman in his cottage, to give serious and earnest consideration to the impressive appeal of the everlasting gospel. By her wise, winsome and essentially womanly ministry, she brought an entire people face to face with Jesus Christ. Henry Venn spoke of her as a star of the very first magnitude; Macaulay said that, if she had been a Roman Catholic, she would have been canonized as Saint Selina; whilst a third authority declares deliberately that she is the greatest woman who has ever lived.

By a singular coincidence, the *man* who, in the whole course of history, did more than any other man for the evangelization of the English-speaking people, and the *woman* who, of all women, achieved most for the same end, passed away within a few weeks of each other. No two individual lives have more profoundly affected our British destinies than the lives of John Wesley and the Countess of Huntingdon. They were both born when the eighteenth century was dawning; despite their prodigious labors and constant anxieties, both lived to a great age; and the eighteenth century was getting ready to die when they went down to their honored graves.

II

Look at her! She is only nine; very pretty; with rosy cheeks, sparkling eyes and a wealthy shock of nut-brown hair. Notwithstanding her great position, her proud title and her exalted rank, she is perfectly natural, exquisitely girlish and entirely free from any suspicion of affectation. Watching her at her play, nobody would suspect that she is the heiress of a noble house that boasts its hoary traditions, its princely lineage and its numerous royal alliances. She is a favorite with her playmates and companions; and all the sparkle dies out of a frolic when the vivacious yet thoughtful little Lady Selina is called to leave it. But, this evening, an unwonted heaviness broods over her gay young spirit. The sprightliness has vanished; she is singu-

larly quiet. She is in no mood for a romp with her
sisters. She walks apart, and, in striking contrast
with her usual reluctance to go to bed, she seeks,
earlier than the appointed hour, the solitude of her
own room. Something must have happened to
cloud her blithe young spirit with such unaccustomed
gloom. It has!

She was out for a walk with her sisters this afternoon when they encountered something that lay
altogether beyond the bounds of all previous experience. They met a village funeral on its way to the
little cemetery on the hillside. The coffin was being
borne along the country road on the shoulders of
four sturdy rustics. Selina's eager mind was all
alert on the instant. Who was it that had died?
It was a child! Did children die? She had never
conceived of such a possibility. And who was the
child? Was it a boy or a girl? It was a girl! With
eyes full of sad surprise the sisters stared at each
other. And was it a big girl or a little girl? How
old was she? She was nine! The other sisters
looked meaningly at Selina; for Selina was nine!
The bright, sensitive child was profoundly impressed. She insisted on their following the *cortège*
at a respectful distance, and they stood near enough
to the open grave to hear every word of the burial
service. The first vague consciousness of mortality
—and immortality—fastened itself upon her mind.
She was a citizen of eternity! There was another
world, and, sooner or later, she would be summoned

to pass into it! She feels this evening that she would give everything—her wealth, her title, her prospects, her all—for some sure hope of happiness in *that* world as well as in *this* one. But *on what foundation can she base such a hope?* That is the question; and, to that question, the poor little Lady Selina can see no possible reply.

She could imagine no reply and she could think of nobody who could help her. At the dawn of the eighteenth century English standards and English manners were at their lowest ebb. Politics had degenerated into an undignified squabble; society was as corrupt as it could very well be; music, art and literature were all degraded; the sports and pastimes of life were universally squalid and often obscene; even religion had become formal, sanctimonious and largely hypocritical. 'The saint,' says Addison, 'was of a sorrowful countenance and generally eaten up with spleen and melancholy.' The parson of the period, as the Countess's biographer points out, was respected for his cloth rather than for his qualities. He sat in the kitchen of the village inn, smoking tobacco and drinking ale with his parishioners, or he played the fiddle in the taprooms of the countryside in the daytime and at the dances and merry-makings at night. He was pinched in means, and was glad to be invited to a meal with the butlers in the servants' hall. A higher class of clergyman went fox-hunting with the neighboring gentry, and cut a brave figure in the social life of the period.

A still higher grade mingled with the wits in the city taverns and coffee-houses. 'But the devout minister of religion was rarely to be met with; the earnest, eloquent, persuasive, energetic, urgent messenger of the gospel was almost unknown.' In what direction, then, could the little Lady Selina look for an answer to her troublesome question? *On what foundation could she base her hope of happiness hereafter?* She called into the void; there was no answer; and the silence mocked her passionate insistence.

III

It is long past midnight. The Lady Selina—now a graceful girl of nineteen—has just returned from the ball. Wearing her beautiful dress, and with her jewels still flashing in her hair, she has thrown herself on her knees beside her bed in a tempest of tears. Never for a moment has she forgotten the tumult of concern that was aroused in her heart ten years ago by that mournful little pageant on the country road. Many and many a time has she stolen away to the cemetery on the hillside, and kneeling beside the grave under the gnarled old yew—the grave of the girl who, in life, she never knew—she has prayed that she may yet find an answer to her question.

And, although no satisfactory answer has reached her, although she is still in the dark as to the true foundation on which the hope of eternal happiness must be based, she has done her very utmost to merit the approbation of the Most High. 'She aspired after rectitude,' her biographer tells us, 'and was eager to possess every moral perfection. In all such matters her Ladyship outstripped the multitude in an uncommon degree. She was rigidly just in her dealings and inflexibly true to her word. She was a strict observer of her several duties in every relationship of life. Her deportment was courteous, her conduct was prudent, her sentiments were liberal, and her charity was profuse. She was a diligent inquirer after truth, and was a regular attendant at public worship.' Yet, for all that, she is uneasy and dissatisfied. She has felt—and never more keenly than to-night—that none of these things provide a solid foundation on which to rest her hope of everlasting felicity.

And, even if they could, there is another question. What of her sin? 'My best righteousness,' she tells us, 'now appeared to be but filthy rags, which, so far from justifying me before God, increased my condemnation. I was filled with remorse, I saw that my heart was deceitful above all things and desperately wicked; and I saw that all have sinned and come short of the glory of God.' This evening she was on her way to a brilliant social function. She is society's darling, the gayest of a gay and distinguished coterie. Wealth, beauty and popularity are all hers. But, for some strange reason, as she was being driven in her splendid equipage to the ball, the old thoughts came surging back upon her. The old question repeated itself again and again. Years before, as a little child, she had memorized the questions and answers of the Westminster Shorter Catechism; and to-night, sitting in her carriage, the first question and the first answer returned to her troubled mind: 'What is the chief end of man?' 'Man's chief end is to glorify God and to enjoy Him for ever.'

To enjoy Him for ever—it was her one desire!

To glorify God—but how?

'I saw,' she cries, 'that all have sinned and *come short of the glory of God!*' Leaving the pleasures to which she had looked forward with such bright anticipations, she hurried home from the brilliant ballroom, and, speaking to nobody as she passed along the hall and up the stairs, she sought the silence of her dainty room. And here she is, charmingly robed and bejewelled, yet weeping as though her heart must break. The old question is as insistent as ever; yet, still, there is no answer. She has relied upon her integrity, her charity, her exemplary behavior; but she feels that she is building upon the sand. *This* is not the true foundation.

IV

The question is answered at last! The beautiful Lady Selina has married into one of the noblest houses in England. She is now the Countess of Huntingdon. And, in marrying the Earl, she has

formed a fast friendship with his sisters, Lady Betty
and Lady Margaret Hastings. By this time strange
things are happening in England. All over the
country men are preaching: they are preaching without a book; they are preaching in fields, on village greens, and by the open roadside. Everybody
is talking about this startling innovation. Moved
by curiosity, the Ladies Betty and Margaret go to
hear the new preachers. They can scarcely believe
their ears. These men talk about religion as if religion really mattered! They speak with fervor,
with urgency, and with wistful entreaty. There are
tears in their eyes as they tell of the love of God,
of the grace of Christ, of the wondrous virtue of the
Cross, and of their own experience of the divine
mercy. The Lady Margaret capitulates unconditionally; her life is transfigured; and she enters into
a gladness of which she had never previously
dreamed. She tells everybody of her radiant experience. Her sister-in-law, the Countess of Huntingdon, is ill; but, sitting by her bedside, the Lady
Margaret tells her that, 'since she had known the
Lord Jesus, and trusted Him for life and salvation,
she had been as happy as an angel!' The Countess
is profoundly impressed both by the words and by
the shining countenance of the speaker. She vaguely
feels that she has found a clue to the baffling problem that has distressed her so long. As soon as she
is allowed a book, she reads carefully the First
Epistle to the Corinthians, always her favorite por-

tion. *'Not many wise, not many mighty, not many noble are called,'* says Paul, in the first chapter of that epistle. 'Not *many!*' 'Oh, how I thank God for that little letter *"m!"* her ladyship used to say. 'Supposing, sitting up in bed, I had read that not *any* noble are called!' She read on until she came to this: *'Other foundation can no man lay than that is laid, which is Jesus Christ!' There* was the answer to her question!

'Since I have trusted in the Lord Jesus Christ for life and salvation,' the Lady Margaret had said, *'I have been as happy as an angel!'*

'Other foundation can no man lay than that is laid, which is Jesus Christ.'

'Now,' says her biographer, 'the day began to dawn! Jesus the Sun of Righteousness arose, and burst in meridian splendor on her benighted soul. The scales fell from her eyes and opened a passage for the light of life. It streamed in, and death and darkness fled before it. When, in her own apprehension, upon the point of perishing, the words of the Lady Margaret had returned strongly to her recollection, and she had felt an earnest desire, renouncing every other hope, to cast herself wholly upon Christ for life and salvation. From her bed she lifted up her heart to her Saviour; all her distresses and fears were immediately removed, and she was filled with joy and peace in believing. She determined thenceforward to present herself to God, as a living sacrifice, holy and acceptable, which, she was now convinced, was her reasonable service.'

'*On what foundation could she rest her hope of eternal happiness?*' she had asked, beside that rustic grave.

'*Since I trusted in Christ,*' the Lady Margaret had said, '*I have been as happy as an angel!*'

'*Other foundation can no man lay than that is laid, which is Jesus Christ.*'

'*Renouncing every other hope,*' her biographer tells us, '*she cast herself wholly upon Christ for life and salvation.*'

That night after the ball she felt that she had been building upon drifting sand; she felt *now* that her faith was founded upon the Rock of Ages.

V

Never was a vow fulfilled more literally, more completely and more cheerfully than the vow that the young Countess registered on that memorable day. '*She determined to present herself to God as a living sacrifice,*' and she did! From that moment to the end of her life she devoted the whole of her private income to the spread of the revival. For the preachers who were driven to the fields and high-ways she built attractive sanctuaries. She called George Whitefield, John Wesley, and other of the flaming spirits of that stirring time, to her drawing-room, and summoned the greatest in the land to hear them. The most dissolute men of the period and the greatest scoffers in the country partook of her hos-

pitality. Princes and peers, actors and poets, statesmen and authors—you can scarcely find one distinguished name in the annals of the time but you will
find that name also among the Countess of Huntingdon's guests. From the moment at which God set
her soul at liberty she had such a thirst for the
conversion of others that she compared herself to a
ship in full sail, scudding before the wind, borne on
by such an influence as could not be described. She
took the movement that was struggling for expression in the highways and by-ways of England
and introduced it into courts and castles. As Cardinal Newman says, 'she opened new worlds to the
revival.' In the nature of things, the Cardinal regarded the Countess as the great high priestess of a
poisonous heresy; but he doffs his hat to her in
spite of everything. He salutes her as one who
simply and unconditionally gave up this world
for the next. She is, he says, an example for all
time. 'She was the representative, in an evil day,
of the rich becoming poor for Christ; of delicate
women putting off their soft attire and wrapping
themselves in sackcloth for the kingdom of heaven's
sake.' The Cardinal finds the whole story 'very
stirring and very touching.' The converts of the
Countess, among both high and low, were innumerable. For whilst, three times a week, she crowded
her drawing-room with the lordliest in the land,
she assiduously visited among the poorest of the
poor. In order to supply the country with a suc-

cession of evangelists, she built colleges, providing in the trust deeds that the men trained under her auspices should be free to join any denomination they liked. As long as she had money she built churches all over the country, and then she sold her jewels to build more. Before our great missionary societies were established she planted missions on the West Coast of Africa, in the South Seas, and among the Red Indians of North America. In order that she might send the gospel unto every creature, she administered her modest household with the strictest frugality, and, at the age of eighty-four, died in debt. She made religion so lovable that the whole nation was sweetened by her influence. In an age in which the atmosphere of the English Court was by no means pure, the King would allow no jests to be made at her expense; and when, one day, Lady Charlotte Edwin broke that rule, the Prince of Wales rebuked her by saying that he would be very glad, on his deathbed, to be able to seize the skirt of the Countess of Huntingdon's mantle.

VI

All this was the superstructure; not the foundation. She clung to her text to the last. *Other foundation can no man lay than that is laid, which is Jesus Christ.* Lest there should be any misapprehension, she put her faith in writing a few months before she died. *'I do hereby declare,'* she said, *'that all my present peace and my hope of future glory depend wholly, fully, and finally upon the merits of Jesus Christ my Lord and Saviour.   I commit my soul into His arms unreservedly as a subject of His sole mercy to all eternity.'*   'There is but One Foundation,' she exclaimed near the end, 'there is but One Foundation on which a sinner like me can rest.'   *That* was the Foundation for which, as a little girl, she had sighed.   She found it in her early womanhood, and, for sixty years, she built upon it bravely.

19

CHARLES SIMEON'S TEXT
1759–1836
Anglican clergyman and founder of
the Church Missionary Society.

Ephesians 3:18

I

CHARLES SIMEON is dead—in more senses than one. His name is seldom mentioned: his works are never read. Yet, for all that, he is one of our epoch-makers and empire-builders and history-makers. To few men do we owe more than we owe to him. Has he not been canonized by the most penetrating, the most illustrious and the most critical of all our ecclesiastical biographers? Sir James Stephen says that if the Church were to revise and correct her standard of personal values, she would mercilessly purge her roll of saints. He points with disdain to many ponderous names in our present calendar. What, he demands, have Saint Dunstan, or Saint George, or Saint Swithin, or Saint Margaret, or Saint Crispin done for us that they should elbow out *Saint Charles of Cambridge?* It is true that he never attained to any exalted rank or dignity; he never achieved any thrilling or romantic exploit to send his name echoing about the world. As a young man leaving college he was appointed to the charge of Holy Trinity, Cambridge; and when death overtook him fifty-four years later, he was still ministering unostentatiously to the same people. 'But,' as Lord Macaulay says, 'if you knew what his authority and influence were, and how they extended from Cambridge to the most remote corners of England, you would allow that his real sway in the Church was far greater than that of any Primate.' So speaks one British statesman; and another, Sir James Stephen, has a passage to much the same effect. 'The splendor of a bishop's mitre pales,' Sir James declares, 'before that nobler episcopate to which Charles Simeon was elevated by popular acclamation. His diocese embraced every city of his native land and extended to many of its most remote dependencies. In every part of the empire he could point to teachers who revered him as the guide of their youth and the counsellor of their later years.' His disciples have become more famous than their master; for many an illustrious name which has become a household word among us would never have been heard of but for the beautiful and potent influence of *Saint Charles of Cambridge*.

Some men make history noisily; you hear, far off, the clanging of their hammers. Circumstanced as they are, it is the only way in which the work can be done. The time is ripe for violent methods and resounding blows. The iron is hot and the anvil stands ready. But whilst the village blacksmith works in one way, the village artist works in quite another. There are men who make history as the sun makes daylight. They are silent as the dawn. Of that quiet company Charles Simeon is the most

distinguished representative. He captivated everybody by the serene calm of his tremendous passion.
It was Charles Simeon's deadly earnestness that so
deeply impressed William Wilberforce. It impressed everybody. Even his critics relented when
they heard him. An earnest man carries at his
girdle the magic key that unlocks all hearts. At his
Sesame every door swings open. Therein lies the
secret of Charles Simeon's amazing and historic triumphs. There he stands in Trinity pulpit, a man
of medium height, with the easy movements of the
trained athlete! His face is cultured and kindly:
his hair is very fair: and in his hazel eyes there is
the suggestion of purposefulness and high resolve.
His style of speech is not prepossessing. His voice
is weak and unmusical; his address is by no means
graceful; and, viewed from some angles, his appearance is a little grotesque. But, as soon as he becomes impassioned, we forget all that. His voice
becomes fervent and compelling: his gestures, becoming more natural as he becomes less nervous,
are expressive of an intense desire to convey the full
force of his argument or appeal: he strikes you as
feeling deeply every word that he utters: his face is
illumined by intensity and pleasant animation.
'Who,' asked Canon Abner Brown, 'who ever heard
a dry sermon from Simeon's lips, or had to listen
to a dull remark in conversation with him?' You
feel that, on the still altar of this man's soul, a great
fire burns. At that fire, torches were lit that dis-

pelled the darkness of continents. But when, and in what way, was that flame itself kindled? *That* is the question.

II

And the answer to that question is that the life of Charles Simeon was dominated, for nearly sixty years, by one sublime passage of Scripture. He was never tired of quoting it. He used to speak rapturously of 'its overwhelming and incomprehensible grandeur.' He was never so happy as when preaching on it. It occurs repeatedly in his correspondence. I must make one or two extracts from his letters. Here is one addressed to Miss Elliott:

'My dear Ellen,' he says, 'Only get your soul deeply and abidingly impressed with the doctrine of the Cross and everything else will soon find its proper place in your system. Labor from day to day *to comprehend the breadth and length and depth and height, and to know the love of Christ which passeth knowledge. That* is all I want.'

Three years later I find him writing to the Rev. J. Venn on the proper discharge of his ministerial duties. Mr. Venn has written stating his difficulties, concluding the list with '&c., &c.' Mr. Simeon urges him, in his reply, to get comprehensive views of *the breadth and length and depth and height, and to know the love of Christ which passeth knowledge.* 'Then,' he asks, triumphantly, 'what will all your &c.'s come to?'

In the *Narrative of Mr. Simeon's Last Illness,* appended to Canon Carus's great biography, we are told that, as soon as he began to fail, his mind turned to his text. 'I am fully determined,' he said, 'to begin at once a set of sermons on that grand subject in Ephesians: *That ye may be able to comprehend what is the breadth and length and depth and height, and to know the love of Christ which passeth knowledge.* I don't expect or desire to *preach* them; but, if my life be spared, *write* them I will!'

A fortnight before he died, he was still harping upon the same theme. 'During the greater part of Thursday,' says Canon Carus, 'his whole mind was absorbed upon his favorite passage: *That ye may be able to comprehend what is the breadth and length and depth and height, and to know the love of Christ which passeth knowledge.* His thoughts were fixed intently on this glorious theme. He declared that he thought that no higher honor could be conferred upon him than to be permitted to prepare for publication a set of discourses on that text. 'It is,' he said, 'the grandest subject I can conceive of. I should think a life well spent in which one wrote four sermons on that passage in a manner worthy of it!' The subject was in his mind all the time.

The text not only dominated him, it *permeated* him. His entire personality became steeped and drenched and saturated with the spirit of it. Acquaintances like William Wilberforce, and historians like Sir James Stephen, were arrested by it. 'Charles Simeon is staying with us,' writes Wilberforce, 'his heart glowing with *the love of Christ*. How full he is of that *love!* Oh, that I might copy him as he copies Christ!' Sir James Stephen speaks of Simeon's life as a triumph of love. 'Slowly, painfully, but with unfaltering hopes, he toiled through more than fifty successive years, in the same narrow chamber and among the same humble congregation, requited by no emoluments, stimulated by no animating occurrences, and unrewarded, until the near approach of old age, by the gratitude and the cordial respect of the society amidst which he lived. *Love* soaring to the Supreme with the lowliest self-abasement, and stooping to the most abject with the meekest self-forgetfulness, bore him onward, through fog or sunshine, through calm or tempest. His whole life was but *one long labor of love*—a labor often obscure, often misapplied, often unsuccessful, but never intermitted, and, at last, triumphant.'

There can be no doubt, then, about Charles Simeon's text. I had, in my congregation at Hobart, an old Quaker gentleman of quaint and charming ways. I knew that he had recently moved, and, chancing to meet him one day on the street, I asked where he now lived. 'Well,' he replied, with a characteristic smile, 'I'm living in the Epistle to the Ephesians!' Charles Simeon dwelt there too.

He made his home in *the love that passeth knowledge*. But what led him, in the first instance, to take up his residence there?

III

Bishop Moule says that Simeon's story of his conversion deserves to rank among our religious classics side by side with the spiritual autobiographies of David, Paul, Augustine, Luther and Bunyan. As a boy at Eton, and as an undergraduate at Cambridge, Charles Simeon was troubled by the thought of his evil and corrupt desires. 'To enter into particulars,' he says, 'would serve no good end. My sins were more in number than the hairs of my head, or than the sands upon the seashore.' He found that it was compulsory, under penalty of expulsion from the University, that he should attend the Lord's Supper. 'My conscience told me,' he writes, 'that Satan was as fit to go as I was,' and he resolved that, since he *must* go, he *must* prepare himself for the awful ordeal. He bought a book— Bishop Wilson on *The Lord's Supper*—and applied himself earnestly to its study. He became much interested in Bishop Wilson's exposition of the story of the Scapegoat. He seemed to see the Jewish priest laying his hands upon the creature's head and confessing over it the transgressions of the people; and he watched the scapegoat, as, bearing the guilt imputed to it, it went to its death in the desert. 'Suddenly,' says Mr. Simeon, 'the thought rushed to

my mind: "What! may I transfer all *my* guilt to
Another? Has God provided an offering for me
that I may lay my sins on His head? Then, God
willing, I will not bear them on my own soul one
moment longer. I will lay my sins on the sacred
head of Jesus." ' This was at Easter-time, 1779; he
was then in his twentieth year.

'On Easter Sunday, April 4,' he tells us, 'I awoke
early with these words upon my heart and lips:
"Jesus Christ is risen to-day; Hallelujah! Hallelujah!" I had as full a conviction that I relied on
the Lord Jesus Christ alone for salvation as I had
of my own existence. From that hour peace flowed
in rich abundance into my soul.' He recognized,
in the Risen Saviour, the Lamb of God who had
taken his sins and borne them completely away.
The love that made such a sacrifice on his behalf
overwhelmed him, as he said, by its incomprehensible grandeur; and he set himself from that
hour *to comprehend the breadth and length and
depth and height and to know the love of Christ
which passeth knowledge.*

He commemorated that unforgettable experience
with each returning Eastertide. 'I look forward
with peculiar delight to Passion-week,' he says,
nearly thirty years afterwards. 'It has always been
with me a season to be remembered, not only on
account of the stupendous mysteries which we then
commemorate, but because, on Easter Day, 1779, I
was enabled, through God's unbounded mercy, to

see that all my sins were buried in my Redeemer's grave.'

'I am happy,' he says in his Diary, on Easter Sunday, 1807, 'I am happy and thankful that the peace which, twenty-eight years ago to-day, flowed into my soul, has never been lost, and that I am as much bent as ever on securing the prize for my high calling.'

'It is now forty years,' he says in 1819, 'since I found peace through the Lamb of God that taketh away the sins of the world. From that time to the present hour I have never for a moment lost my hope and confidence in my adorable Saviour.'

And, not long before his death, he wrote in the margin of his Bible a solemn pledge never to forget that Easter Sunday, 1779, on which his deliverance was completed.

IV

Charles Simeon's text is the text of the *Four Magnitudes*: '*to know the love of Christ which passeth knowledge.*' The *Breadth* of it! the *Length* of it! the *Depth* of it! the *Height* of it! It is, as a Roman Catholic expositor has said, '*wide* as the limits of the universe; *long* as the ages of eternity; *deep* as the abyss from which it has redeemed us; and *high* as the throne of God itself.' 'Immensity is,' as Dr. Dale finely says, 'the only adequate symbol of its vastness.' Charles Simeon explored all four of these dimensions.

He scaled the heights. As you follow him through the pages of Canon Carus's great biography, you seem to be watching some patient mountaineer as he steadfastly ascends the rugged slopes. Time after time he reaches a point that he had mistaken for the summit. There is always a peak towering above him, beckoning him on and on and on. There is always a height beyond the height. Great as were the discoveries of the love of Christ that Simeon made, he found that love still incomprehensible to the very last. It was always beyond him.

He sounded the depths. He tasted heavy losses, crushing sorrows and bitter persecutions. At one stage of his career at Holy Trinity, the parishioners locked up their seats, undergraduates broke up the services, and Mr. Simeon was insulted whenever he ventured on the streets. He bore it all uncomplainingly, and, many years afterwards, told of the anguish through which he then passed. 'One day,' he said, 'when I was an object of much contempt and derision in the University, I strolled forth, buffeted and afflicted, taking my little Greek Testament in my hand. I prayed that God would comfort me with some cordial from His Word; and opening it, the first text which caught my eye was this: *They found a man of Cyrene, Simon by name; him they compelled to bear His cross.* Simon, you know, is the same name as Simeon. It was the very word I needed. What a privilege—to have the cross laid on me to bear it with Jesus! It was enough! I could leap and sing for joy! "Lay it on me, Lord!" I cried; and henceforth I bound persecution as a wreath of glory round my brow.' However deep the abyss, the love of Christ was always beneath him.

He explored the breadths. He felt that the love of Christ was vast enough to embrace the whole wide world. He, therefore, became one of the founders of the Church Missionary Society; and, not content with this, set himself to raise up a generation of missionaries. For years he gave a tea-party once a week to which nobody was personally invited, but at which all young men from the University were welcome. Every Friday evening his rooms were thronged. The gatherings became historic. From that tea table there went forth men who, in all parts of the world, made their names illustrious and renowned. As the Bishop of Calcutta said at the time, 'the last day alone will reveal the aggregate of good he thus accomplished. If we take, as examples, only four or five cases—David Brown—Henry Martyn—John Sargent—Thomas Thomason—and Bishop Corrie—we may judge by them, as by a specimen, of the hundreds of similar instances which occurred during the fifty-four years of his ministry.' He always spoke of his tea-party men with a faltering of the voice and a moistening of the eye. As an old man of seventy, he glanced over a list of the names of the men who, during the

forty years between 1789 and 1829, had been most
successful in missionary work in India. 'Why,' he
exclaimed with delight, 'they are all of them my
tea-party men!' He ever afterwards referred playfully to India as 'my diocese.'

And he investigated its length. Or, at least, he
is investigating it still. For, as Bernardine à Piconio
has already told us, it is long as the ages of eternity.

V

The story of his death, which occupies several
pages, is one of the most exquisitely beautiful nar-
ratives of the kind on record. 'Well, sir,' said
Canon Carus, as the end approached, 'you will soon
*comprehend what is the breadth and length and
depth and height and know the love of Christ that
passeth knowledge!*' 'Ah,' the dying man exclaimed,
with rapture, 'I shall soon understand that text
now!' A little later, seeing that Mr. Simeon was
fast sinking, Canon Carus pronounced over him the
Aaronic benediction: *'The Lord bless thee and keep
thee: the Lord make His face to shine upon thee and
be gracious unto thee: the Lord lift up His countenance upon thee and give thee peace!'* The dying
man smiled, folded his hands, whispered a faint
Amen, and never spoke again. 'The like of his funeral,' exclaimed one astonished spectator, 'was never
seen before, and never will be seen again. More
than fifteen hundred gownsmen attended to honor
him.' 'He went down to his grave,' says Sir James

Stephen, 'amidst the tears and the benedictions of the poor, and with such testimonies of esteem and attachment from the learned as Cambridge had never before rendered even to the most illustrious of her sons.' And why? Simply because he had, by his lovely life, helped men to *comprehend the breadth and length and depth and height and to know the love of Christ which passeth knowledge.*

20

THOMAS WINGFOLD'S TEXT

Clergyman in George MacDonald's novel
The Curate's Awakening.

Matthew 11:28

I

AT dead of night—and of a winter night at that—
the young minister sat on a gravestone in the
churchyard, vainly attempting to answer two tremendous questions. *Ought he to resign?* that was
the *second* of the two; and the *first* was even more
momentous. The Reverend Thomas Wingfold was,
according to George MacDonald, the curate in
charge of the Glaston Parish Church. He did not
quite know *why;* he had often wondered. He had
caught himself one morning sitting beside the stream
in Osterfield Park, pondering that strange problem.
Why was he a minister? He noticed that the sun
shone without knowing *why* it shone; the wind blew
without knowing *why* it blew; the waters babbled
over their gravelly bed without knowing *why* they
did so; and he seemed to be living his life on precisely the same principle. For him, the ministry
had always been part of the programme. He was to
go from home to school; from school to Oxford;
and from Oxford into the Church. He had neither
applauded nor resented it; he had simply abandoned
himself to the inevitable. It was his destiny. He
felt it his duty to yield his personality to all the

heights and hollows of the mould into which he
was being thrust. The Church was an ancient institution of undoubted respectability; she possessed certain emoluments and required certain observances;
why should he hesitate to serve her? The work was
not distasteful. The visitation of the sick was irk-
some to him, it is true; but, on the other hand, he
enjoyed the musical side of the services; and he was
able to meet the demands of the pulpit in virtue of a
parcel of manuscripts—old, yellow, and respectable
—which his uncle, a Doctor of Divinity, had con-
siderately bequeathed to him. And Thomas Wingfold, a young fellow of six and twenty, might have
laid out the whole of his life on this plan had there
not come to him hurtling through the smoke of a
companion's cigar, a staggering and unanswerable
question. It was the *first* of the two questions that,
in the quiet churchyard, he sought to solve. And it
was that *first* and major question that had started
the *second* and minor one.

It was George Bascombe who had raised it.
George was a brilliant young barrister—and a sceptic. 'Everybody who knew him counted George a
genuine good fellow, and George himself knew little
to the contrary. See him!—tall and handsome as an
Apollo and strong as a young Hercules; dressed in
the top of the fashion; self-satisfied, but not offen-
sively so; good-natured; ready to smile; as clean
in conscience, apparently, and as large in sympathy,
as his shirtfront!' George Bascombe visited Glas-

ton; he and the curate met one evening at the same
table; and a companionship sprang up between them.
In the course of a walk one day the two young men
passed the church. George looked at it and smiled,
a little scornfully. The curate sought an explana-
tion of the sneer.

'Well, I will be honest with you,' George replied;
and, stopping abruptly, he turned square towards his
companion and took the full-flavored Havana from
his lips. 'I like you,' he went on, 'for you seem
reasonable; and besides, a man ought to speak out
what he thinks. So here goes! *Tell me honestly—
do you believe one word of all that?*'

'The curate,' George MacDonald says, 'was taken
by surprise and made no answer; it was as if he had
received a sudden blow in the face.' He evaded a
direct reply; and, as a result, the question—as such
questions will—rushed back upon him in his hours
of solitude. That accounts for our finding him here,
at dead of night, his brow bathed in perspiration,
with these two questions taking it in turns to torment
him.

Do I really believe the things that I preach?
Is it my duty to resign my charge?

He reminds himself that he has done his best; he
had entered the ministry under a sense of duty;
and had conscientiously met its obligations. But it
is cold comfort. 'It remained a fact that if Barrister Bascombe were to stand up and assert in full
congregation that *there was no God* anywhere in the

universe, he, the minister of the parish, could not, on the Church's part, prove to anybody that there *was.*' He could not even think of a single argument on his side of the question. 'Was it even *his* side of the question? Could he say *he believed* there was a God?' That was the question—the question that George Bascombe had asked him once, and that he had since put to himself a hundred times; the question that he could not answer; the question that had raised another.

Did he believe?

Should he resign?

He suddenly discovered that a gravestone on a November midnight is a cold chair for a study; he rose, stretched himself disconsolately, almost despairingly; looked long at the dark outline of the old church and at the tombstones huddled about him; and, utterly miserable, went home.

II

Happily, the world is not made up of clerics and infidels. Thomas Wingfold and George Bascombe were not the only people in Glaston. Every village contains a few oddities peculiarly its own; you cannot imagine such people living anywhere else. The oddities of Glaston were a couple of dwarfs—Joseph Polwarth and his niece Rachel. Within the stunted and unshapely body of Joseph Polwarth, however, there dwelt a cultured mind and a beautiful soul. The dwarf was very poor but he sometimes visited the parish church and occupied one of the free seats. He soon discovered that the sermons that the curate was preaching were not his own; they were copied, holusbolus, from the works of Jeremy Taylor. The dwarf knew that nobody else suspected it, he therefore resolved to guard the secret jealously. He knew nothing of the curate's indebtedness to his dead uncle; but he vaguely felt that the minister was sinning ignorantly rather than wilfully; he therefore wrote a kind and courteous note, drawing his attention to the matter. The discovery of his uncle's dishonesty, and of his own complicity, intensified considerably the wretchedness of Mr. Wingfold's position and added to the difficulty of his course. Moreover, it raised again the old question. *Did he really believe?* If he really believed, would he have had need of such pitiful makeshifts and desperate expedients as these?

In his extremity he sought the assistance of his accuser. He went to see the dwarf, and, attracted by the little man's transparent sincerity and ready sympathy, poured out his heart to him.

'What shall I do? he cried, in closing his sorrowful confession. 'How am I to know that there is a God?'

And then the dwarf threw a new light on the entire situation. He urged the minister to lay less stress on the poverty of his *intellect* and to pay more heed to the hunger of his *heart*. The question is, he said, not *Is there a God?* but *If there be a God, how am I to find Him?* The best possible evidence of the existence of God would be—to know Him! And then he told of his own experience. He, too, had had his days of darkness and of doubt. He had read everything that came within his reach, and nothing had helped him. Then it occurred to him that, in common fairness, he ought to read the New Testament from cover to cover.

'I began,' he said, 'but did not that night get through the first chapter. Conscientiously, I read every word of the genealogy; but when I came to the twenty-third verse and read *"Thou shalt call his name JESUS; for he shall save his people from their sins,"* I fell on my knees. To tell you all that followed, if I could recall and narrate it in order, would take hours. Suffice it that from that moment I was a student, a disciple. I had found the man Christ Jesus, and in Him had found the Father of Him and of me. My dear sir, no conviction can be got, or, if it could be got, would be of any sufficing value, through that dealer in second-hand goods, *the intellect.* I know only one way of proving to yourself that there is a God, and that way is Jesus Christ as he is revealed to the heart that seeks Him.'

Jesus! Jesus! Jesus!

Jesus, the Saviour from human sin!

Jesus, the Revelation of the Heart of God!

The minister felt that the key that would turn the two locks of his dungeon, the secret that would solve both his questions, had been placed in his hands.   On the next Sunday he confessed from the pulpit that the manuscripts that he had been reading were not his own; and, even before Sunday came, he had set out, like the wise men of an older time, to find JESUS.

III

Like the magi following the star, the curate followed the glimmer of light that the dwarf had pointed out to him. And, like the wise men's star, it led him to the Saviour.   He was being tormented one day by the old, old questions:

Do I believe the things I preach?

Is there a God?   How can I tell there is a God?

Shall I give up?   Must I resign?

When, suddenly, a great and golden text shone, like a burst of sunlight, across his misty path.   'The words arose in his mind: *Come unto Me, all ye that labor and are heavy laden, and I will give you rest.* His heart filled.   He pondered over them.'

'I know only one way of proving to yourself that there is a God; and that way is Jesus Christ!' the dwarf had said.

'*Come unto Me, and I will give you rest!*' said the text.

He came!   He, the curate, knelt at the feet of the Crucified. And, on the following Sunday, the whole congregation felt that the minister had suddenly become very sure of God.   For he preached, and preached as he had never done before, from the words *Come unto Me, all ye that labor and are heavy laden, and I will give you rest.* 'Come, then,' he said, as he drew to a close, 'come and see whether His heart cannot heal thine. He knows what sighs and tears are; and, if He knew no sin in Himself, the more pitiful must it have been to Him to behold the sighs and tears that guilt wrung from the tortured hearts of others. Let us get rid of this misery of ours. It is slaying us. Here is One who says He knows; take Him at His word. Go to Him who, in the might of His eternal tenderness and human pity, says: *Come unto Me, all ye that labor and are heavy laden, and I will give you rest!'*

IV

Every village has its tragedies as well as its oddities. At Glaston there dwelt Helen Lingard. It was at her home that George Bascombe and the curate had met; for George was laying siege to Helen's heart. And Helen had at home a brother, Leopold, who was slowly dying, and dying with the awful sin of murder on his hands. In a frenzy of passion and jealousy he had stabbed his sweetheart. Helen was at church that morning, and, on her return, she hurried to Leopold's bedside.

'I never saw such a change on any man as there is on Mr. Wingfold,' she said. 'Do you know, he preached as if he actually believed the things he was saying, and not only that, but as if he expected to persuade us of them too. His text was *Come unto*

Me, and I will give you rest, a common enough text, but somehow it seemed fresh to him and he made it look fresh to me. Just think, Poldie,' she added, passionately, 'just think! What if there should be some help in the great wide universe somewhere—a heart that feels for us both as my heart feels for you! Oh, wouldn't it be grand! If there should be Somebody somewhere who could take this gnawing serpent from my heart! *Come unto Me,* he said. *Come unto Me, all ye that labor and are heavy laden, and I will give you rest.* That's what he said; oh, if it could be true!'

And sometimes, when all the doors between his bedroom and the drawing room were open, Leopold heard Helen at the piano singing the 'Comfort ye,' from *The Messiah.* And once when she came to the words: *Come unto Me, all ye that labor and are heavy laden, and I will give you rest,* she broke down; and then, with sudden resolution, she raised the top of the piano, began again, and sang the words as she had never sung them in her life.

'Helen,' said Leopold, a few days later, 'I have been thinking all day of what you told me on Sunday.'

'What was that, Poldie?'

'Why, those words of course—what else? *Come unto Me, all ye that labor and are heavy laden, and I will give you rest.* You sang them to me afterwards, you know. Helen, I should like to see Mr. Wingfold.'

It was the one thing that Helen had most wished to avoid. Under the minister's influence, Leopold might reveal his guilty secret, confess his crime, and whelm the family in shame! Mr. Wingfold came, however, and they talked about the text. The minister soon found that nothing calmed and brightened the dying man like a talk about Jesus.

'When,' Mr. Wingfold said one day, 'when He was in the world, He said *Come unto Me, all ye that labor and are heavy laden, and I will give you rest!* It is rest you want, my poor boy, not deliverance from danger or shame, but rest, such peace of mind as you had when you were a child. Come to Him! Ask Him to forgive you and make you clean and set things right for you! If He will not do it, then He is not the Saviour of men and is wrongly named *JESUS!*'

Leopold hid his face. But he yielded at last, accepted the great invitation, confessed his dreadful sin, and found the peace that passeth understanding.

And so did Helen. She was talking one day to her sceptical lover.

'*You* need no God,' she said, 'therefore you seek none. If you *need* none, you are right, I dare say, to *seek* none. But *I* need God—oh, I cannot tell how much I need Him!—and I will go on seeking for Him to the last!' She sought the curate's help, and he pointed her to Jesus. It is the only way. The magi—the scientists of an older time—had

searched the universe for finality, for truth, for
God. They found all that they sought at Bethlehem.

V

'Is there a God?' asks the scepticism of my soul
within me and the scepticism of the world around.

'Search for Him!' replies the wise little dwarf at
Glaston, *'and when you find Him you shall know!'*

'Come unto Me,' says the text, going one step
further, *'Come unto Me, all ye that labor and are
heavy laden and I will give you rest!'*

It is sound philosophy. What is it that Principal
Shairp sings?

> And must I wait till science give
>   All doubts a full reply?
> Nay, rather, while the sea of doubt
> Is raging wildly round about,
>   Questioning of life and death and sin,
>   Let me but creep within
> Thy fold, O Christ, and at Thy feet
>   Take but the lowest seat;
> And hear Thine awful voice repeat
> In gentlest accents, heavenly sweet:
>   Come unto Me and rest;
>   Believe Me and be blest!

'Come unto ME!' says the Saviour. Religion is
intensely and essentially personal. Till we find
HIM we are groping among the fogs of November:
when we find *HIM* we are in the sunshine of June
and, having found Him, can never seriously doubt
again.

21

LORD SHAFTESBURY'S TEXT

1801–1885

Evangelical social reformer and member of parliament.

Matthew 25:44–45

I

LORD SHAFTESBURY'S text was emblazoned, bit by bit, on the craped banners that were borne in his funeral procession. When the *cortège* turned into Parliament Street, on its way to Westminster Abbey, a sight was witnessed which, as Mr. Edwin Hodder says, can never be erased from the memory of the generation that beheld it. London, the city that has gazed upon so many solemn pomps and stately pageants, had never seen such a funeral. From the moment at which the coffin emerges from the home at Grosvenor Square, till the moment of its arrival at the Abbey doors, the great black crowds stood bareheaded in the driving rain to do honor to one who had made the world a happier place for everybody in it. Lord Shaftesbury had literally clothed a great people with spontaneous mourning, and was going down to his grave amid the benedictions of the poor. The most destitute and degraded had somehow contrived to procure a little tatter of black to wear upon the coatsleeve or in the bonnet; for every individual in that immense throng felt dumbly the poignant anguish of a personal sorrow.

The coffin, when it lay in the Abbey, was buried beneath masses of the most exquisite flowers. There were ornate wreaths from the crowned heads of Europe, and there were bunches of violets from the children of the ragged schools. Some of these fragrant tributes had been sent by princesses, and some by flower-girls; some had come from the homes of statesmen and some from the homes of costermongers; some from palaces and some from alms-houses; some from millionaires and some from crossing-sweepers, shoe-blacks and newsboys.

But the incident—the outstanding incident—the incident that can never be forgotten—the incident that brings into dramatic and striking prominence Lord Shaftesbury's text: what was it? Let Mr. Hodder tell his own story. 'As the funeral *cortège* passed into Parliament Street,' he says, 'a sight was seen which will never be forgotten while this generation lasts'; and he proceeds in graphic language to describe it. Grouped on the east—or river—side of the street were deputations from Homes and Asylums and Refuges and Schools and Societies and Training Ships; indeed, from all the Missions and Charities which, like flowers in the springtime, had sprung into existence under the magic of Lord Shaftesbury's influence. Each of these grateful groups bore a banner hung with crape; and on each banner were emblazoned some such words as these: *'I was an hungered and ye gave Me meat'*: *'I was thirsty and ye gave Me drink'*: *'I was a stranger*

and ye took Me in': 'I was naked and ye clothed
Me': 'I was sick and ye visited Me': and 'I was in
prison and ye came unto Me.'   Bands of music, play-
ing the Dead March, were ranged at intervals, and,
as the procession passed, these, heading the deputations with their eloquent banners, fell in and marched
towards the Abbey.

There, then, on the banners, stands Lord Shaftesbury's text! And if, that day, Lord Shaftesbury
could have spoken, he would have said, *'Lord, when
saw I Thee an hungered, and fed Thee? or thirsty,
and gave Thee drink? When saw I Thee a stranger,
and took Thee in? or naked, and clothed Thee? or
when saw I Thee sick or in prison, and came unto
Thee?'*   And the answer would have consisted of
the old familiar words: *'Verily, I say unto you,
inasmuch as ye have done it unto the least of these,
my brethren, ye have done it unto Me.'*

II

Lord Shaftesbury's religion, like his text, was intensely *personal*. The emphatic word in the text,
the astonishing word, the word that elicits a startled
reply, alike from the righteous and the wicked, is the
personal pronoun.

'I was an hungered and ye gave ME meat!' says
the Voice from the Throne, approvingly.

'When?' cry those upon the right hand in surprise, *'when saw we THEE an hungered and gave
THEE meat?'*

'I was an hungered and ye gave Me no meat!'
says the Voice from the Throne, reproachfully.

'When?' cry those upon the left hand in surprise,
*'when saw we THEE an hungered and gave THEE
no meat?'*

'Inasmuch,' replies the Voice from the Throne,
*'inasmuch as ye did it unto the least of these, ye did
it unto ME!'*

*'Inasmuch as ye did it not unto the least of these,
ye did it not unto ME!'*

In the light of those revealing words, all life is
reduced to a series of transactions between the individual soul and the individual Saviour. Nothing
is impersonal. Everything that I do, I do to *Him;*
my neglect is always the neglect of *Him;* in *Him* I
live and move and have my being. The secret of
Lord Shaftesbury's life was a profound recognition
of this pervasive and penetrative truth. To him the
living Christ—the Christ who died and rose again—
was everything. 'My faith may be summed up in
one word,' he used to say, 'and that one word is
Jesus.' In season and out of season he pleaded with
the churches to give the people the gospel. 'I believe,' he said, 'that the sole remedy for all our distresses is one of the simplest and one of the oldest;
the sole, the sovereign remedy is to evangelize the
people by telling the story of the Cross on every occasion and in every place. In the stateliest cathedral
and at the corner of each common street, in the
royal palace and in the back slums, we must preach

Christ to the people: we must determine, like Paul, to know nothing among men save Jesus Christ and Him crucified. I believe with all my heart that He, and He alone, is the power of God unto salvation.'

In private life, as in public, it is always the same. His journal is punctuated with entries such as this:

March 30, 1866. Again saw Henry Sturt. He was full of the same confidence, calm and resigned. *'Christ died for every one,'* he said, *'and for me.'* Here he realized the highest point of Christian life in appropriating to himself, in faith and love, the merits of our Lord and Saviour.

Lord Shaftesbury's faith is nothing if not *personal*. Christ and he—he and Christ—deal at first-hand with each other. How did so sublime an understanding come into existence? On that point there can be no uncertainty at all.

III

The angel of Lord Shaftesbury's pilgrimage was Maria Millis. She was only a servant, a simplehearted, affectionate Christian woman, true as steel to every conception of duty. 'She formed a strong attachment to the gentle serious child,' the biography tells us, 'and would take him on her knee and tell him Bible stories, especially the sweet story of the Manger of Bethlehem and the Cross of Calvary. It was her hand that touched the delicate chords of his soul and awoke the first music of his spiritual life.' It was Maria Millis who taught him the first prayer that he ever learnt; he used it constantly in later years: and, in his old age, and particularly in times of sickness, he very frequently found his tongue involuntarily framing those simple words. 'In her will,' we are told, 'she left him her watch, a handsome gold one, and until the day of his death he never wore any other.' He was fond, even to the last, of showing it. 'That,' he used to say, 'was given to me by the best friend I ever had!'

'She told him the sweet story of the Manger of Bethlehem and the Cross of Calvary!' And thus she introduced him—a frail little lad of seven—to a Friendship that grew more intimate, more potent and more fruitful as life went on.

IV

William Law says that, if one looks at the way of the world, one would hardly think that Christians had ever read the twenty-fifth of Matthew. It is a grave indictment. If, however, the religion of Lord Shaftesbury is, like his text, intensely *personal,* it is also, like his text, intensely *practical.* It is one of the most grievous tragedies of the spiritual realm that the soul sometimes finds the sunny climate of an ardent evangelism singularly enervating. The faith is sound yet nothing comes of it. Nobody can level such a charge against the evangelism of Lord Shaftesbury. Like his Master, he went about doing good. How could it be otherwise when his life was modelled on such a text? The finest comment ever made on this great passage in Matthew was penned by Lord Charnwood in his *Life of Abraham Lincoln*. Lord Charnwood remarks that 'in the most moving and the most authentic of all Visions of Judgment, men were not set on the right hand or the left according as they were of irreproachable or reproachable character: they were divided into those who *did* and those who *did not.*' '*Inasmuch as ye did it . . . ye did it unto Me!*' '*Inasmuch as ye did it not . . . ye did it not to Me!*'

The same thought was always uppermost in the mind of Lord Shaftesbury. Take a typical instance from the record of his mature life. It is a beautiful Sunday afternoon in the autumn of his fifty-eighth year. Lord Shaftesbury is spending a quiet hour with his Bible. It is open at the twenty-fifth of Matthew. He has read that noble passage a hundred times before but it acquires new interest with each perusal. Having carefully weighed and pondered every word, he rises, reaches for his journal, and sets down his impressions. Here they are:

Oct. 11, 1857. Read this afternoon Matthew xxv. What a revelation of the future judgment of the human race. Those on the left hand are condemned, not for murder, robbery, debauchery, not for breaches of the decalogue, or for open blasphemy, not for sins they have committed, but for duties they have omitted. Men say '*I have done no harm*'; I am not worse than my neighbors; and so on. But God takes another view. '*Have you done good?*' He asks.

It was because Lord Shaftesbury recognized these twin aspects of his text—the intensely *personal* and the intensely *practical*—that he became the greatest doer of his time. *'Inasmuch as ye did it,'* says the text, and Lord Shaftesbury's claim to immortality rests on the fact that he *did things*. The record of his achievements fills a volume of eight hundred pages. In the mines and the factories, in the prisons and asylums, among the waifs of the city and the toilers on the rural farms, he effected reforms by which life was simply transfigured. Existence for countless thousands was scarcely tolerable until he came to their relief. He revolutionized the whole industrial world. His figure became the most familiar, the most commanding and the most honored in the public life of England. He was singularly good-looking; tall, slender and extremely graceful. His form was statuesque in the perfection of its poise and proportions. His head, with its handsome face and its clusters of dark curling hair, was reminiscent of a classic bust. Whether addressing the House of Lords or talking to the ragamuffins of a London slum, he was always heard with the most profound respect. 'My Lords,' exclaimed the Duke of Argyll, in a great political speech delivered in 1885, 'the social reforms of the past century have not been due to a political party: they have been due to the influence, the character, and the perseverance of one man: I refer, of course, to Lord Shaftesbury.' 'That,' said Lord Salisbury, in commenting upon the Duke's statement, 'is, I believe, a very true representation of the facts.' No more convincing proof could be desired that a true believer must, in the nature of things, become a great achiever. Lord Shaftesbury's text says so.

V

The spiritual world is divided into two hemispheres—the *Mystical* and the *Material*. They are both represented in the text: and, for that reason, they are both reflected in the life and labors of Lord Shaftesbury. The one, if properly cultivated and developed, leads naturally and inevitably to the other. Even Goethe, in his *Parable of the Three Reverences,* taught us as much. Wilhelm Meister, the reader will remember, tells Natalia of the strange and mysterious land which he had visited. The children in the fields greeted him with three kinds of gestures. The first class looked cheerfully up to the sky. These, he was afterwards informed, represented reverence for things *above* them. The second class looked round upon the beauty of the world. These represented reverence for things *about* them. The third class stood with downcast eyes. They represented reverence for things *beneath* them. Wilhelm desired further enlightenment, and was taken by the chief to a kind of Palace Beautiful. In the *first* apartment he finds exquisite representations of Old Testament story. The interpreter explains to him that this place is sacred to the *First Reverence*—reverence for things *above* us. These stories, he says, have done more than anything else to inculcate that lofty sentiment. In the *second* chapel he meets equally beautiful representations of New Testament incidents. He is told that he is now in the place sacred to the *Second Reverence*—reverence for things *about* us. The New Testament, he is told, has done more than anything else to inspire that veneration. Then, moving along the corridors, Wilhelm comes to a closed door. He asks to be admitted to the sacred precincts of the *Third Reverence*—the reverence for things *beneath* us. But it cannot be. The chief explains that the chapel of the *Third Reverence* is a Sanctuary of Sorrow, and only those who have been deeply taught in the First and Second Reverences can be admitted into that temple of tears. It is a perfect allegory. One has not to know much of the world in order to learn that, when one comes into contact with men and women, he is laying his hand on a quivering underworld of heartbreak and of anguish. And only those who have been profoundly instructed in the Old Testament Reverence for things *above* them, and in the New Testament Reverence for things *about* them, are qualified to look into those pitiful faces and those streaming eyes. It was because of those old Bible stories that Maria Millis had so often unfolded to him; and it was because, at her feet, he had caught the spirit of that sweet story of the Manger of Bethlehem and the Cross of Calvary, that Lord Shaftesbury was able, in later years, to embark upon his wonderful humanitarian ministry.

VI

It was thus that the text made Lord Shaftesbury the greatest practical mystic of all time. He was essentially and instinctively a mystic. He saw Christ where nobody else discovered Him. As a lover hears his lady's name in the sigh of the wind and the song of the birds, so, having learned to love his Saviour with all his soul, Lord Shaftesbury found Him everywhere. Sir Launfal found Christ in the leper. Lord Shaftesbury saw Him in criminals, orphans, cripples, paupers, lunatics and chimney-sweeps. He spent all his time, his fortune and his energy on *them,* because he felt that, inasmuch as he did it unto *them,* he did it unto *Him.* Thus, I find him at dead of night in a thieves' kitchen. Look at him! He is surrounded by hundreds of the most desperate criminals in London. They listen respectfully as he urges them to abandon their lawless lives. 'But how,' one burglar wants to know, 'how are we to live if we give it up?' Lord Shaftesbury urges them to pray for guidance. 'But, my lord,' one man replies, 'prayer is very good, but prayer won't fill an empty stomach!' The objector evidently mistook Lord Shaftesbury for a mere dreamer of dreams. He did not know his man. Lord Shaftesbury took the names of those who sincerely desired to live honestly, and within a few months he had settled hundreds of them on Canadian farms or introduced them to honorable and remunerative avocations at home.

Pray!—there stands the *Mystic!*
An Emigration Policy—he is a *Practical Mystic!*

VII

On his twenty-seventh birthday, Lord Shaftesbury deliberately pledged himself in writing to seek two things—*the honor of God* and *the happiness of men.* When, many years later, Mr. Gladstone was asked to draft an inscription for a monument to Lord Shaftesbury, he said of him that 'he devoted the influence of his station, the strong sympathies of his heart and the great powers of his mind to *honoring God* by *serving his fellow-men.'* Now what are these two things but the twin factors that we have discovered embedded in the text? They colored his entire career. Learning every day to love his Saviour a little more devotedly and learning every day to serve his fellow-men a little more effectively, he wove the pattern of that great text into the fabric of a singularly winsome and useful life. There is no more to be said: the supreme business of life is to follow his lead.

22

DR. R. W. DALE'S TEXT
1829–1895
English Congregational minister and education reformer.

John 14:1–2

I

IT was the veteran's last struggle. Dr. Dale lay dying. And, in dying, a horror of great darkness fell upon him. He who had established the faith of thousands found his own faith failing him. Happily he lived long enough to conquer and to tell the secret of his victory. The Rev. George Barber sat by his bedside at Llanbedr, and, into his ear, the sick man poured the story of his conflict.

'It was a sad, distressful night in the early stages of my illness,' the doctor said. 'The house was quiet, all the members of the family having retired to rest. Soon after midnight I awoke in great pain, and a terrible distress crept over me. I was full of fear. I did not wish to disturb my wife and daughters; they were worn out with anxious watching; so I lay silently struggling against the indescribable horror of an unknown dread. When the conflict reached its worst it seemed as though Christ Himself came, and, standing close beside me, said: *Let not your heart be troubled; ye believe in God, believe also in Me. In my Father's house are many mansions; if it were not so, I would have told you; I go to prepare a place for you.*' 'That,' added the doctor, with a look in his face that was full of noble confidence and glorious hope, '*that* steadied me, and I felt strong and safe in the love of Christ.'

I am not surprised. Every minister knows that the experience is a very common one. 'Whenever I am called to a house of sickness or sorrow,' said Ian Maclaren, 'I always read to the troubled folk the fourteenth chapter of John. Nothing else is so effective. If a man is sinking into unconsciousness, and you read "*In my Father's house are many mansions,*" he will come back and whisper "*mansions,*" and he will wait till you finish "*where I am there ye may be also*" before he dies in peace.' Nor is this Ian Maclaren's only tribute to the spiritual charm of the familiar verses. For, in one of the most affecting scenes in any of his writings, he again introduces the passage that he found so potent in his own ministry. In 'The Doctor's Last Journey,' Drumsheugh reads the deathless sentences at the deathbed of Doctor Maclure, the truest soul in Drumtochty. 'It's a bonnie word!' exclaimed the dying doctor. And, turning back to history once more, everybody remembers that, in those last sad days at Abbotsford, Lockhart read the self-same chapter to Sir Walter Scott. 'It's a great comfort,' sighed Sir Walter, 'a very great comfort!'

'*Let not your heart be troubled: ye believe in God, believe also in Me. In my Father's house are many mansions: if it were not so, I would have told you: I go to prepare a place for you.*'

'*That steadied me,*' says Dr. Dale, '*and I felt strong and safe in the love of Christ!*'

'*It's a bonnie word!*' exclaims Doctor Maclure.

'*It's a great comfort,*' sighs Sir Walter Scott, '*a very great comfort!*'

And all three of these testimonies were uttered on the brink of eternity.

II

Let nobody suppose, however, that these monumental words were designed for the special consolation of *the dying*. Such an assumption would be the very reverse of the truth. They were first uttered by the dying for the special consolation of *the living*. The Redeemer of the world was turning His face towards the Cross, and was comforting the desolate hearts of His disciples. He was bracing them to serve and to suffer; He was guarding them against the paralysis of despair. The ministry of these great words to *the dying* has been one of the most arresting experiences of the Church; but it is in their ministry to *the living* that they achieve their most splendid triumphs.

A few years ago, eighteen million people in the United States set themselves to a systematic study of John's Gospel. Dr. W. T. Ellis commented on the circumstance in the columns of the *Boston Transcript*. He describes the sensual, pleasure-loving, materialistic and decadent old city of Ephesus—the city in which the words were written. He pictures

the members of the Ephesian Church imploring the
aged John to commit to paper the sacred and beautiful memories with which he had so often fortified
their faith and enriched their hearts. And he points
out that 'the little company of devout disciples,
whom even the corruption-laden air of a great
heathen capital could not enervate, little dreamed,
when they besought their aged pastor and spiritual
father to write down his personal memories and his
interpretation of Jesus Christ, that the biography
penned by John would one day be studied in five
hundred languages, and that it would become the
text of special study for millions of persons in continents then undreamed of.' In regard to the con-
tents of the book, Dr. Ellis mentions only one passage. It is not *'God so loved the world . . .'* or *'Him
that cometh unto Me I will in no wise cast out.'* It
is *'Let not your heart be troubled.'* 'Peep,' says Dr.
Ellis, 'into any mature Christian's copy of the Bible
and it will be found to open most naturally at the
fourteenth chapter of John's Gospel, where the best-
thumbed passages will be seen to be those beginning: *"Let not your heart be troubled."* Beyond
a doubt, this old book, which springs like a white
lily of spirituality out of the black mud of Ephesian
heathendom, is the most popular and the most help-
ful bit of writing to be found in all the world.
Myriads and millions of persons, of all sorts and
conditions, have found it a veritable book of life.'
Now this is extremely significant. We are to peep,

be it observed, into the Bible of a *mature Christian:* this mellowed believer has not yet come to the valley of the shadow; it is in the rough and tumble of *life* that he has found the words so precious. They form 'a veritable *book of life,*' Dr. Ellis maintains. The experiences of the ages would amply vindicate his conclusion. We must go into the matter a little more thoroughly.

III

From a great cloud of witnesses I select two as typical. Both are members of a colored race. One is from history, one from fiction. One is a woman, the other a man.

Dr. Grattan Guinness was here in Australia when, in July, 1906, he received the sad news of the death of his daughter, Lucy. 'Never,' wrote Mrs. Guinness, 'can I forget his tearless grief as he read the cabled message of sorrow. He sought comfort in solitude, and went away to a quiet bay on the shore of New South Wales. A few Australian aborigines were living there. One morning, as he sat with bowed head listening to the mournful music of the sea, a hand was laid on his shoulder, and, in the strange accent of the aborigines, he heard the familiar words: *Let not your heart be troubled; ye believe in God, believe also in Me. In my Father's house are many mansions; if it were not so I would have told you.* He looked up and saw at his shoulder the wrinkled face of an old colored woman, shining with a heavenly light. She was God's messenger to him. On the following Sunday he preached a sermon on Faith which those who heard will never forget.'

Poor Tom—the hero of *Uncle Tom's Cabin*— would not object to being placed in the company of this Australian aboriginal. The two have much in common. Tom is being carried by the slave-boat up the Mississippi. He has been sold. He looks back over the stern of the vessel and seems to see the old Kentucky farm with its shadowy beeches; seems to see the master's house, with its wide cool halls; seems to see the little cabin overgrown with multiflora and bignonia. He seems, too, to see Aunt Chloe, his good wife, busy in her preparations for his evening meal; he seems to hear the merry laughter of his boys at play; he seems to be listening to the chirrup of the baby at his knee. And then, with a start, it all fades, and the horrid reality rushes back upon him. 'Is it strange,' Mrs. Beecher Stowe asks, 'is it strange that some tears fall on the pages of his Bible as he lays it on the cotton-bale, and, with patient finger, threading its slow way from word to word, traces out its promises? Having learned late in life, Tom is but a slow reader, and passes on laboriously from verse to verse. Fortunate for him is it that the book on which he is intent is one which slow reading cannot injure; nay, one whose words, like ingots of gold, seem often to need to be weighed separately, that the mind may take in

their priceless value. Let us follow him a moment
as, pointing to each word and pronouncing each
half-aloud, he reads:

*'Let—not—your—heart—be—troubled. In—my
—Father's—house—are—many—mansions. I—go
—to—prepare—a—place—for—you.'*

'Cicero,' adds Mrs. Stowe, 'Cicero, when he buried
his darling and only daughter, had a heart as full
of honest grief as poor Tom's; but Cicero could
pause over no such sublime words of hope, and look
to no such future reunion.'

Here, then, is our Australian aboriginal quoting,
for the comfort of a strong man bowed down by his
sorrow, the words that she has learned at the mis-
sion-station. And, as a result, he rises, pulls himself together, and, a few days later, preaches a
sermon which fortifies the faith of all who hear it.
And here is poor Uncle Tom, not dying but living,
finding in the same rich cadences a tonic and an
inspiration that brace him to face the bitter realities of a slave's existence.

'That steadied me,' says Dr. Dale, with Death
spreading his sable wings above him, *'that steadied
me, and I felt strong and safe in the love of
Christ!'*

'That steadied me,' says Uncle Tom, reeling under
the bludgeonings of circumstance, *'that steadied me,
and I felt strong and safe in the love of Christ!'*

Whether a man is looking into the face of *Death*
or into the face of *Life,* it is all the same. In either

case, those words are equally precious. They are
like ingots of gold, as Mrs. Beecher Stowe puts it.
'They are bonnie words!' as Doctor Maclure exclaims. 'They are a great comfort, a very great
comfort!' as Sir Walter Scott sighs, gratefully.
When Hugh Sutherland, the young tutor, told old
David Elginbrod that he had just lost his father,
the old man reached down the Bible and read the
fourteenth of John as Hugh had never heard it
read before. When he rose to go, David walked
home in silence beside him. 'The spirit of his
father seemed to accompany them. Hugh felt that
the sting of death had vanished—the sepulchre was
clothed with green things and roofed with stars!'
Those golden words contain all the stimulus that a
man needs in facing the stern realities of this life;
they contain all the solace that he needs as he con-
fronts the gathering shadows that haunt the portals
of the life to come.

IV

The things that I most enjoy are the things that I
find it most difficult to define. I cannot even describe
my own delight in them. How can I set down in
words the pleasure that I find in the perfume of a
violet, in the song of a thrush, or in the graceful
poise of a deer? In the same way, how am I to explain the appeal that these majestic and gracious
words make to my heart? It is impossible. I can
expound neither the words themselves nor the emo-

tions that they excite. I only know that the fragrance of the violet is very sweet; that the song of the thrush is a rapture to the ear; that the dappled deer, standing with head erect and foot upraised, holds my eye entranced; and that the great words of the text, recited in my hour of need, flood all my soul with comfort and with courage.

'Let not your heart be ruffled, disturbed, distracted,' the Saviour says; 'ye believe in *God*, believe also in *Me*.' It is such a mistake to set the one thought over against the other.

'I find it easy to believe in *God*,' writes Cyril Makepeace, in a letter that the postman brought me not very long ago. 'When,' he goes on, 'when I recite the creed, the first clause seems so perfectly natural and fitting: *"I believe in God the Father Almighty, Maker of heaven and earth."* How can I look at the universe around me without believing in God, the Maker of it all? But *Jesus*! *"I believe in Jesus Christ, His only Son, our Lord."* I find it very difficult, in my thought and devotion, to find room for the figure of *Jesus*—the pale Jew of a lone Syrian town—within the compass of my conception of God.'

And, over against this feeling of Cyril Makepeace, I place the difficulty of Mary Fairfax. Mary came to me one evening in great trouble.

'It is so easy,' she exclaimed, 'to believe in *Jesus*. How can anybody read the New Testament without believing in Him? But *God*! Oh, how I wish that

I could really believe in *God!* To me, *God* is so
incomprehensible. How can anybody love *God?*'

Poor Cyril Makepeace! Poor Mary Fairfax!
'Let not your heart be distracted by such distinctions,' says the text. 'If you can nestle your aching
heads in the *Father's* love, be glad; do not let the
technicalities of the faith disturb your peace. If
you find comfort in the thought of *Jesus,* make the
most of it. *"He that hath seen Me,"* He said Himself, *"hath seen the Father."* Why set the two
thoughts in antagonism in the day of tears?'

The heart and the intellect must not quarrel in the
hour of grief. If the *heart* is in the sunshine, let
the intellect range itself beside it and share the genial
glow; if the *intellect* sees the way shining through
the gloom, let the heart unquestioningly follow!
Let there be no clash, no discord, no inner turmoil.
*'Let not your heart be troubled; ye believe in God,
believe also in Me.'*

> 'Twas the Master Himself who said it
>   To the sorrowful little band,
> Facing an hour of darkness
>   That they could not understand.
> The light of their lives was fading.
>   Their eyes with tears were dim,
> The rugged men were shaken
>   At the thought of losing Him.
>
> 'Let not your heart be troubled.'
>   Never was voice so sweet.
> Never was look more kingly,
>   Nor assurance more complete.

'Let not your heart be troubled,
    Ye believe in God Most High,
And one with God the Father,
    Equal with Him am I.'

'That steadied me,' said Dr. Dale, *'and I felt strong and safe in the love of Christ!'* With so brave a testimony on record, other staggering minds will know in which direction to look when the shadows close thickly about them.